"In an ever-increasing noisy world where overwhelm seems to be the norm and pain the output, one can find hope in the perspectives of *Jounce*."
        - Geoff Flamank, general manager of E-xact Transactions, Vancouver, B.C.

"Brosseau's *Jounce* is a meaningful, personal, and purposeful journey. He hurdles the abyss of hollow inspiration; it's action that's needed. More than ever the stewardship of our communities and planet is in desperate need of fostering a greater collective spirit of care. Brosseau masterfully connects language with the spirit of mobilization."
        - John F. Gray, technology entrepreneur, writer, teacher

"In simple and concise language, Jim gets right to the essence of the complexity of how our mind relates and reacts to the chaotic world unfolding around us. He provides an insightful framework on how we may live a life of fulfillment in this fast changing world. When we understand, accept and resolve the tension between our inner experiences and the objective outer realities, we are better able to make the important life decisions that are right for each of us. It is a must-read for anyone who seeks purpose and a clear direction in life."
        - Marina Ma, managing director, MMA Consulting Inc.

"This is a practical guide to the Hero's Journey. Jim uses personal story to set the conditions of 'The Call' the moment in our lives when something terrible happens to awaken us to the fact that the cultural world we live in is not suited for life. We, of course, can hear and obey this call or not. Jim shows us that the consequences are dire if we do not. The book then moves to a series of pragmatic steps that enable us to take charge of our own lives and so escape the life-damaging story of the modern culture."
        - Robert Paterson, author of *You don't Need a Job You Need a Trust Network*

Jounce

Jim Brosseau

Jounce

*Crafting a resilient life in an
increasingly chaotic world*

ISBN 978-0-9939031-0-6
First printing: November 2014

To Winney,
who helped me understand that this was really my way
of grieving after all

What is Jounce?

If our change in position over time is *Speed*, and our change in speed over time is *Acceleration*, and our change in acceleration over time is *Jerk*, then our change in jerk over time is *Jounce*.

Jounce is a real term in physics. Though seldom encountered in science class, we often go through life being *jounced*, jerked around in several directions at once. From a traffic ticket to bad news from your doctor to a global catastrophe, the sources for being *jounced* are all around us.

This book is about dealing with *Jounce*.

Contents

Preface

This book started brewing in my head six years ago, when I had been hit by a perfect storm of events; I had been quite heavily jounced. Initially, I was very angry, but over time, through reflection and conversations, my perspective mellowed.

I learned that even if I cannot control the world around me, I am still able to influence how my life turns out. I have the capacity to lead the life I want to live, while navigating my way around whatever it throws at me.

I learned I am on a journey, and have been all my life without being conscious of that fact. Now I am learning how to consciously direct my journey to be more fruitful and have more value.

I have no illusions that my journey exactly mimics yours. I have gained some insights and skills that I share in this book, more as examples that have worked for me than as specific activities you need to mimic. You won't find a specific recipe for success in these pages, as I don't think one exists.

Introduction

You will find, in the first section, some observations about the world around us that may feel a bit dark for what is meant to be an uplifting book. I do believe that we are reaching a point where there are some very dark clouds on the horizon, many of our own making. This perspective is intentional, as I've found we need to clearly see those storm clouds if we are to actually do anything about them. I want this book to be a call to action.

The actions you take, though, need to be your own. This book is a walk through my experience, and tries to put some structure around an approach to life that will make the most of our journey and help us work through the difficult times. Some ideas will resonate with you, and you should feel free to use them as you see fit. This is an unfinished expression of my journey to date. You will have viewpoints, ideas, and conclusions of your own that will add to my views to make the result richer and more real for yourself.

With the guidance provided by this book, you can start to build that more resilient life; imagine a rich, vibrant vision for where you want your life to go; consciously choose the steps required to get there. With intention, you will move away from merely drifting around, subject to the jounce of the chaotic world around you. You will move toward what you want rather than being frozen with uncertainty or running from what you fear. You will create a more enjoyable journey, regardless of the destination you choose.

If this book helps you see and interact with the world in a different way, that's a start. If this book helps you decide you can choose to make a difference in your own life and the lives of others, even better. If you make use of some of the tools I'm offering to help you to lead a richer, more resilient life, you're welcome. If this book becomes the start of a conversation where we both grow and learn from one another, we have both won.

In any case, be conscious of your journey.

Notes

While I have a few perspectives that are unique to me, the vast majority of what is in these pages comes from other people. To keep things conversational, I've avoided citing too many research ideas or models in the book itself. There are no graphs to interpret, no tables to wade through. There are Chapter Notes at the end of the book if you wish to explore any ideas further, as each topic merits deeper study on its own.

One of my goals for this book has been to avoid diving too deeply into scientific models or theories. This has been difficult at times, as there are many models and theories I lean on in different ways to help me understand the world around me, and I threw the essence of all of them into a big melting pot here.

In the workplace I've learned the best way to get a point across is to tell a story. It will help people internalize what they have learned. Only afterwards can you divulge what the model was that you had in your back pocket to guide the conversation.

If you lead with the model, you have merely provided a lightning rod for people to argue against.

Virtually every topic in this book has a great depth of research behind it; the book merely scratches the surface and introduces the ideas. Sometimes there are conflicting opinions about what is 'right' for a given topic, a sure sign we are all still learning.

Becoming a student of the world around us is a great tool to help understand what we perceive, and at times to adjust our views accordingly. Physician and author Edward de Bono once said, "If you never change your mind, why have one?"

At the beginning of each chapter is a song that has resonated with me in the past. I've found music and lyrics can be a useful tool to share thoughts, emotions, and ideas. You may not be familiar with all of these tunes, and I'm sure you can readily come up with a replacement that resonates better with you, in any genre of music that you enjoy.

Part I - A Chaotic World

The world we live in is presenting us with a wider range of challenges than ever before.

We are depleting our planet's resources to the point of exhaustion while wedging more people into its limited space.

The structures of civilization aren't scaling up to serve the needs of the growing masses and are buckling under conflicting priorities.

We are trying to get more done in less time, resulting in short tempers and superficial relationships.

On top of all that, we are bombarded with more distractions to indulge in as an attempt to escape the insanity around us.

Chaos manifests itself differently for every one of us, and there are plenty of forms of it to go around. At times it appears all the elements of our world are conspiring against us, driving us to the brink, jouncing us from our staid lives. This section explores these elements in more detail.

our joyous lives are tenuous threads

Billy Walker

Fragile – Sting, 1987

The early 70s in rural Southern Ontario was a simpler time than we live in today. There was no Internet and social media to connect us 24/7 with our friends; news of the world took days to reach us; our sphere of music consisted of a few albums and what the local radio stations carried. We didn't peer into the lifestyles of the rich and famous, and reality TV was still thirty years away. As long as we were home for meals we could come and go as we pleased – to fly kites in Centennial Park, play a game of baseball with all those McAuliffe kids (the games never seemed to end without a quarrel), or head out to the back forty to get stuck in the mud or choke on a cigarette that one of us had stolen from our parents.

We would go fishing out on the lake or wander around the local ponds catching frogs. Those were the days when we could stroll into Mrs. Mears' store with a dime and load up on Pixie Stix or Chocolate Soldiers and get all wired up on more sugar than should be legal for kids of our age.

Our parents' lives didn't seem to be much more complex. Dad was a carpenter who worked union hours, Mom waitressed once in a while, and used most of her time raising eight kids. They spent evenings and weekends watching TV, playing cards with neighbours, or taking us out on the lake to fish or swim; even long-distance calls were a rarity. We would get our dose of world news at six o'clock or eleven every evening. But our lives were largely centered on our neighbourhood.

Boyhood friends

I remember Saturday afternoons in the Walkers' living room, watching Sir Graves Ghastly – an old actor in a cheesy vampire costume who would introduce old scary movies with giant ants or creatures with zippers up the back. Billy had Creepy Crawlers and a black light and he introduced me to Alice Cooper. Billy was cool and a bit bigger than me, both great reasons to have him as a friend.

We got into trouble once in a while, as eleven-year-old kids often do.

One winter day, we were horsing around in our yard, throwing snowballs at one another, and Billy really let one fly. He might have whiffed his throw or I might have ducked just at the last minute. Either way, the window behind me didn't survive the impact.

My dad was furious and banned Billy from our yard. I don't recall the duration of the sentence that Dad handed down, but we knew it was in our best interests to lay low for a while.

Some time later that same winter, we were in Billy's yard playing in a snowstorm. We got to talking about our situation, the fact that our territory had become so horribly constrained to, well, pretty much anywhere in the neighbourhood *except my yard*. This was totally unacceptable to us, and it was time to head over to feign an apology to Dad.

That was the evening of March 4th, 1972. The snow was blowing hard and it was already dark. There were no streetlights along our stretch of road, and visibility in the blowing snow wasn't all that good.

Billy and I were bundled up in snowmobile suits, big boots, and gloves, with our hoods pulled up over our toques and scarves. We could play outside for hours like that, protected against the cold. If it got really blustery, we would cinch our hoods up against the wind, which made it a bit more difficult to see. I don't recall the colour of the snowmobile suit I was wearing, but I do know that Billy's was black.

Shattered

I crossed the highway first, and turned back just in time to catch a glimpse of what happened. I'm sure I saw more, but self-preservation and the passage of time have served as effective erasers.

I don't remember if I had brazenly run in front of that vehicle with little time to spare, as kids tend to do. But I do know that Billy ran right into the side of a car driving along the highway, likely into the rear view mirror on the driver's side. I probably heard the impact. I saw the car slide out of control and into the nearby ditch. I saw Billy lying in the middle of the road, thrown a bit further down from where we were crossing.

What happened that night after Billy got hit is mostly a blur, but shards of memory still remain.

I remember the driver saying he never saw Billy, and that is probably true. I remember talking to a policeman that night about what happened. I remember taking some time off school, though I don't know if it was days or weeks. My family tells me that I was in a state of shock, which really wouldn't surprise me.

I remember that evening how my older sister Joyce came tearing out of our house to try and help. She was in nursing school at the time, but I don't think she had any real hope of saving Billy that night. Running into the side of a fast-moving car can wreak havoc on a kid's body, and my guess is that the snowmobile suit merely managed to hold everything relatively together. I seem to recall a stain on the road for a long time after that, though I could be mistaken.

One thing that really stands out for me was my return to school. I can still clearly see the kids' faces against the backdrop of the new wing they added to the school, all those faces staring at me. It's funny how you recall some things like that.

The big thing I remember was how they all just gawked at me and left me alone. Apparently, once word had gotten around about the accident, well-intentioned parents suggested that their kids don't talk to me about what happened to Billy.

I find that most of us are reluctant to talk about death, and I can't recall a single instance of anyone bringing up Billy in conversation again during my childhood. This silence didn't help me process what had happened that night in 1972.

I vaguely recall Joyce taking Billy's passing very hard, how she took responsibility for it in some way. Joyce finished nursing school, and spent most of her career as an emergency-room nurse, where you never know what you are going to run into during your shift, and you learn that modern medicine simply can't save everyone.

I managed to move on, though interacting with the Walker family was always awkward after that night. While Billy's and my parents were always neighbourly to one another, our families had never been close friends, and over time it seemed that Billy's family became more and more isolated from the community. I expect their run of bad luck had something to do with it; they had lost an older son in a train accident a few years before Billy's passing.

I try to imagine how Billy's family managed in the years that followed his death. I know our children are a huge part of our lives, probably the key part of the legacy we are leaving in this world. We want the best for them, we certainly don't want their lives cut short before they can experience their joys and leave their own marks. Despite the challenging experiences involved in raising two headstrong, bright kids, my wife and I would be crushed by such a loss.

Over the years, I made new friends and life went on. I think about Billy less and less over the years, and when I recall him today, it's more about the fun times we had than the final evening that ended his life.

I may be a little too cautious when I watch my own kids crossing the road these days. I'm sure this is one of the ways that evening long ago changed me.

No one is immune

As we go through our lives, we can all expect to encounter events that have a huge impact on us. It may be the loss of a loved one, or a major illness or accident that we struggle to recover from. We may fail to achieve something that is important to us, or we may become one of the many people who are downsized from their jobs.

We hear about massive storms that take the lives of thousands of people, or plane crashes, or other catastrophes around the world, events that may touch us personally.

In many ways, those old, simpler times I recall from my childhood are gone for good. The world is becoming more crowded, more complex, and more dangerous. Change is happening at an accelerating pace we are struggling to keep up with. Part of this, of course, is that we get older and gain more responsibilities. But there is more to consider.

Even if we live what people would call a charmed life, where everything goes our way, we still have the end of our lives to contend with – death and taxes, as the old saying goes. Some people, like Billy's family, seem to have runs of bad luck. Superstition says that bad things come in threes. There are people who never seem to be able to catch a break.

Misfortune often hits us without any advance warning, whether it is a deep loss or a small setback. While there might be writing on the wall sometimes, we generally ignore those signs. We can't prevent these events from happening or predict what will come, and they don't have to be as severe as the examples above to strongly impact our lives.

As I struggled with the death of a best friend when I was eleven, I had family and friends watching me closely, helping me through the crisis. From my point of view, though, I was simply adrift, unaware of what I could do to make things better, and I could only endure until the pain went away.

I'm sure my life has taken a different path as a result of those events over forty years ago, and I have had to deal with other crises in my life as well. Often, we don't even realize that we can make a choice, and we don't recognize that our way of dealing with challenges can cause us more harm than good.

My sister Joyce dealt with other crises in her life as well. By August 2008, it had all become too much for her, and she took her own life.

As you can imagine, our entire family was shocked by Joyce's passing. We progressed through all the stages of grief, and we all worked through that tragedy in different ways. At the time, I was already down, recovering from pneumonia, and this news set me back quite a bit. Sometimes, it feels as though life is ganging up on us.

In the six years since then, I have studied how we deal with tragic events and small setbacks in our lives, and have learned some useful skills to help me regain my footing and return to a positive, constructive outlook. I am learning that we can be more proactive about seeing those signs – the writing on the wall that we tend to ignore. I have found there is strength in numbers and we can work together to become stronger.

While events can change us, they do not have to drag us down. We can choose how to deal with calamities that unfold in our lives. There are things we can do to help ourselves see situations more clearly, find positive outcomes, and get back on our feet. Even without knowing what dark events lurk around the corner for us, we can prepare ourselves and make ourselves more resilient.

Reflections

What major setbacks have you dealt with in your life? How long
did it take to get through the challenges to land on your feet?

What challenges are you currently struggling with? How do
you feel about your skills to work through these difficult times?

we live in a time of accelerating change

Swirling in Transition

What's Going On – Marvin Gaye, 1971

We can think of our dance with the world as different layers of impact.

The first layer, the one I describe in this chapter, is the *environment*, the world around us. It is the result of billions of years of formation of our universe, millions of years of evolution, and ultimately, the onslaught of information and the increasingly rapid pace of change we are swirling in at the moment. While we may have some small influence on how this unfolds, for the most part we need to accept that this is the environment we live in. This environment, in turn, defines much of the path that we, for better and for worse, are destined to follow.

There are other, closer layers that impact us.

The next layer is the *institutions* that support our daily lives: governments and industries such as banking and the medical infrastructure that simplify our lives and allow us to get things done. As the population in the world grows, we are starting to see cracks in the infrastructure of these institutions.

Environment
Institutions
Relationships
Perceptions

Our vulnerable lives

Layers that impact us

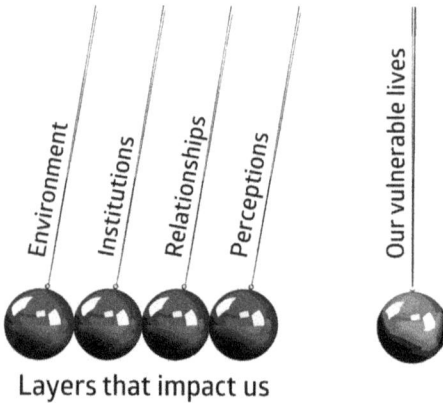

After institutions comes the layer of *relationships* we have with others; call it our neighbourhood. This is how we interact with the people who are closest to us, and how their actions and the events around us impact us directly. We have much more influence at this layer than we do with the first two.

The closest layer to us involves how we see ourselves and how we manage our own *perception* of the outer layers. For most of us, most of the time, this is not a conscious process, and we are often overwhelmed by our emotions and feelings to a degree where we don't feel we are in control.

Although we need to examine what we – starting with ourselves – can do from the inside to build resilience, I will describe these layers of impact from the outside in.

We're falling behind

When we first evolved from apes, we had our fair share of challenges, to be sure. At that time, most of those challenges centered around struggles to find enough food to survive and to avoid things that wanted to eat us.

Gradually, very gradually, our world changed. We started to get organized, learned to use tools, and became more efficient at protecting and sustaining ourselves. We became hunters and gatherers, and found safety in large groups. In fits and starts, our numbers grew. We leveraged our opposing thumbs and our pre-frontal cortex to become masters of our environment, rather than merely eking out an existence. We have evolved over millions of years, and we are still evolving today.

Until recently, an evolutionary process that takes many generations was good enough; the pace of change was, literally, glacially slow. There was no appreciable change in the world around us within our lifetime, or even within generations, and evolution easily kept up.

Not so today; the world we live in is changing faster than ever.

We harnessed fire a couple million years ago. More recently, we invented the wheel, created new ways to hunt for food and kill one another, developed better agriculture techniques. We have been able to leverage our newfound skills and drastically change the world around us in leaps and bounds.

In the past couple of centuries, we have seen the invention and distribution of electricity, the Industrial Revolution, the transistor, and the various technologies that have followed. We have also seen the invention of the atomic bomb, all the good and bad that comes with being connected globally, and an explosive growth of people trying to survive on this planet. It took all of our history to reach a world population of one billion by the early 1800s, and only about 130 years to double that. We are now over seven billion people, way more than double the number that was on the earth when I was born.

These huge changes are happening within our lifetime. Many of them have been a huge benefit to us, allowing us to thrive, explore the arts, and experience leisure time. And the pace of change will continue to accelerate. Slow evolutionary adaptation just can't keep up.

But we are seeing more changes that don't fit this mold. With so many people on the planet, the overcrowding and conflicting ideologies are creating new challenges. Resources that fuelled the industrial revolution are becoming scarce commodities, and conflicts across the globe are becoming more commonplace and more deadly. The events of 9/11 have made it clear that religious strife is no longer contained within the borders of distant lands.

This sandbox we live in is too crowded, and there is no longer any corner where we can contentedly play by ourselves. While Europe, Africa, and Asia have lived with everything from feudal conflicts to epic battles for centuries, we realize that we are all deeply interconnected and struggling in a new era of survival.

A change in the weather

The Industrial Revolution, with all its benefits, has driven us to burn fossil fuels at such a scale that we are actually changing the world climate. There is plenty of evidence, if we choose not to ignore it, that global temperatures are rising as a result of the greenhouse gases we are spewing into the atmosphere. Many scientists characterize it as 'global warming', and because of its world-wide implications, I can't recall anything that has polarized people so strongly into two camps: those who recognize it as at least plausible, and those who don't want to believe the compelling evidence that it is already happening.

Here on Canada's West Coast, it seems the winters have been milder, and the summers and autumns in recent years have been glorious. From where I sit, maybe this global warming thing isn't all that bad. For now.

I recognize that where I live is but a small outpost, and that 'global warming' is better described as 'climate change'. From that view, while the climate in my backyard may seem to be improving, I can also appreciate the challenges we are facing, with species dying off, glaciers retreating, ice shelves breaking away, and precipitation patterns changing drastically. We are seeing a frightening increase in the frequency and size of storms that hit different parts of the world in different seasons. Hurricane Katrina struck the U.S. Gulf Coast in 2005, Typhoon Haiyan decimated the Philippines in late 2013, to name just a couple.

Haiti experienced a devastating earthquake in 2010, Japan is still reeling from a tsunami in 2011, and we are still waiting for 'The Big One' in our neck of the woods. While earthquakes aren't traditionally considered the result of human impact, there is evidence that our desperate fracking practices do contribute to increased seismic activity.

We are pushing this planet well beyond its capacity, and Gaia is starting to push back.

Information overload

We are also growing more aware of these events, though even the biggest of disasters gets elbowed off the front page in a couple of days. Many people still remain displaced by Katrina, but that is no longer newsworthy. The results of the leaks in those nuclear power plants in Japan are still unfolding several years later, but this too has become less important than the latest celebrity scandal.

With changes coming at a faster pace, we are being bombarded with more information than ever before. I grew up with teachers and textbooks, a library card, and a set of beat-up, old Encyclopedia Britannica at home as my sources of knowledge. These have been replaced by the Internet, which didn't exist for most of us before the early 1990s. Newspapers are suffering from a smaller subscriber base and struggling to adapt, but generally not very well. Magazines are generating online content, and squeezing it into digestible chunks that we can read on our phones or reference in our Tweets or on Facebook or Pinterest.

By the time this book is published, some of these references will already be outdated, but the message remains the same: The number of information sources is escalating daily, and the quality of this information is being diluted. While Wikipedia does a great job of reviewing and managing its quickly evolving content (old encyclopedias were meticulously researched and written and static), the World Wide Web in many ways is like the Wild, Wild West. Anyone can post their opinions on the Web, and most people do, including myself. Few readers take the time to verify the authenticity of this information.

Like most people, I have searched the Web to learn about some ailment I've got, only to find it might be anything from an innocent rash to terminal cancer. I've encountered situations where my kids will describe something they consider factual, only to find that they learned about it on someone's blog, or in a reader's comment on an otherwise carefully monitored medical site.

The world is changing faster than we can evolve and we are ill equipped to adapt to these changes. We are being hit with more, less credible information than we can hope to process.

Toto, we are definitely not in Kansas anymore.

Our response

For all of the issues I talk about here, there are various ways of responding to them.

We can certainly do our part to behave in a responsible manner. We can all reduce-reuse-recycle and shrink our footprint on the planet. For those things that are within our control, we can consider the impact of our decisions before we act. We can keep a disaster kit available in case we need it. We can think before we accept anything we read on the Web as gospel, and we can be more sensitive to the information and opinions we post online to make sure we don't merely add to the noise drowning out valuable messages.

For greater impact, we can support areas in need through volunteerism. We can donate generously to worthy causes. We can devote our careers to research, or to efforts to make the world a better place.

Solutions such as these are not for everyone, though, and few of us have the resources of a Bill Gates that could make a dent in what is happening around us. Most of us, for most of our lives, have little impact on what is happening on a global scale. For that, what might make the most sense is to reflect on the first part of the Serenity Prayer:

> God grant me the serenity to accept the things I cannot change;
>
> courage to change the things I can;
>
> and wisdom to know the difference.

We don't need to believe in a higher deity to learn from this; that's not the important part. What is important is to recognize that there are critical events happening in the world today. If we aren't prepared to make the effort to have an impact on them, we need to simply accept them. Continued fretting over them will not help. Let it go.

We need to first get a handle on how we see ourselves and manage our own perspective on the world. Then, we gather a set of tools that we can use to manage our daily lives, effectively keeping ourselves together. Once we have our own ducks in a row, we are better equipped to interact within our neighborhood – to be of value to others and deal with institutional deficiencies.

Reflections

You don't need to have experienced my particular observations to see that the world is becoming more complex and changes are happening faster than ever before. What are the events you have seen that might bring you to the same conclusions?

On the flip side, what are the events you have observed that lead you to see things in a different light?

the illusion of support increases our burden

Our Failing Institutions

For What It's Worth - Buffalo Springfield, 1967

It used to be that we lived our lives surrounded by a range of trusted institutions. These were put in place with common structures to govern and protect the people, manage our businesses and resources, and nurse us back to health when we were sick. These institutions were run for the people by the people – you and me and our neighbours and friends. While run by individuals, they existed for the greater good of the masses.

I'm pretty sure it hasn't happened all at once, and it may be that over time I am simply gaining a deeper understanding of what is really going on in the world, but I am seeing that there is a real decay in these institutions. While originally focused on the common good, our supporting infrastructure is losing its focus on the people. Like layers being peeled off a huge onion, there are more signs all the time that society's interest in the common good is disappearing. This is a source of stress for many of us.

Who benefits from medicine today?

Take the medical field, for example. Western medicine has long been touted as a miracle, with many debilitating diseases being overcome, new technology to effectively diagnose what ails us, and the design of new and revolutionary medications that can make us more comfortable and prolong our lives. This same Western medicine, for all that it has done to improve our lives, remains what has been called 'the youngest science' by physician and author Lewis Thomas. This youngster appears to be having some growing pains.

Forty or fifty years ago, it was quite common in many areas for doctors to make house calls. Today, at least in North America, there is a shortage of physicians and it can take days or weeks to get an appointment for five minutes of your doctor's time. Wait times for surgeries or transplants can easily stretch into several years. The house call for most of us is a thing of the past.

There is increasing pressure to support more and more people with fewer professionals. The medical system compensates physicians (who have often racked up huge debts in med school) on a per-patient basis. Put these two together, and it is not surprising that there are many doctors and walk-in clinics that appear to run their businesses like an assembly line.

The result is doctors spending less time diagnosing the root cause of problems, with little time taken to explain to the concerned patient what they believe is going on, and a tendency for them to lean more and more on prescribing medicines that often merely mask the symptoms rather than addressing the root cause. As in many disciplines, this short-term focus actually has a negative long-term impact on the industry. People behave based on how they are rewarded, and for doctors, like many others, cash is king.

Another factor that plays a role here is the arrogance of many people in the medical industry (and other institutions), the attitude that 'we absolutely understand what we are doing!'

Sorry, Doc, but I would tend to disagree, based on what history tells us and what I have seen.

I have no doubt that modern medicine has a solid grasp on how to deal with physical ailments. Reset a broken bone, repair a ligament, remove a wart – all pretty straightforward things to manage, even with the complexity of the human body. Medicine is also pretty strong at managing many of the chemical imbalances in our systems, either through diet or supplements, and we have a growing awareness that much of the food we consume is over-processed and filled with ingredients intended to make us eat more rather than to make us healthy.

It is in the area of the electrical systems of the human body where I believe the arrogance of the medical profession is getting us into trouble. A key outcome of that imbalance between supply and demand in medicine is a tendency to write a prescription for drugs that are intended to help us think straight and be happy, productive, 'normal' citizens, rather than understand and manage underlying root causes.

The number of children and adults being diagnosed with 'mental disorders' has been rising dramatically in recent years, and of those who are diagnosed, an expanding number are being treated through medication rather than through more labour-intensive psychotherapy. Our definition of what is 'normal' is narrowing accordingly.

In *Medication Madness*, the author Dr. Peter Breggin asserts that there was a forty-fold increase in children being diagnosed and treated for bipolar disorder between 1994 and 2003, with 90% of these children being treated with medication. More than 47% were being treated with antipsychotic drugs, none of which were approved for children. Antidepressant use doubled in the U.S. between 1996 and 2005.

Speaking from experience

I've seen first hand what can happen with today's medications.

Our family learned after Joyce committed suicide that over a period of four years she had been exposed to a long line of different antidepressant medications, more than a dozen that we are aware of. The general approach in prescribing drugs that affect our brain is to start with a very small dose under close supervision, as clinical studies show that patients respond differently in different circumstances. If the medication is found to not produce the desired effect, the tapering off should be just as controlled and supervised. In Joyce's case, she was at least a couple of times taking several medications at once. Were all these different combinations vetted through clinical trials? Given the large number of medications on the market today and the cost of clinical trials, likely not.

In my dealing with the tragic loss of a loved one, there was a brief period after Joyce's death that I too struggled with depression. While I believe we have one of the better family doctors around, given the pressures of the industry, we eventually got to the point where he cautiously raised the possibility of taking prescribed drugs.

At my wit's end, I gingerly proceeded. I started with a very low dose, and for a while things seemed to get better. Not only was I managing to get through the day with more of an upbeat tone, I was able to achieve more than I had done in the recent past. And that's when it dawned on me – the day I was talking to one of my sisters on the phone while folding the laundry and doing about eight other things at the same time. (Me doing housework should have been the first sign for concern.) I wasn't depressed any more. I had swung all the way across the spectrum from depressed to manic.

These drugs, even at minimum dosages, can be scary things. Many have 'black box warnings' about potential side effects, such as depression and suicidal thoughts, the very maladies that most of them were formulated to manage in the first place.

I had dreams about suicide a few nights later, and stopped taking the pills cold turkey, rather than tapering down. That brief roller-coaster ride was one I have no interest in getting back on.

Pharmaceuticals is big business worldwide. It can take years and millions of dollars to bring a new drug to market, and like most corporations, the big pharmaceutical manufacturers are in the game for profit. They are primarily beholden to the shareholders, and the big, successful companies are indeed very big and very successful.

There have been several documented cases in the news where big pharma companies are being fined huge money for overstepping the rules of the game. But they consider it part of doing business. In 2009, for example, Pfizer was fined $2.3 billion for illegal drug promotions that 'plied doctors with free golf, massages, and resort junkets', to get them to prescribe drugs for 'off-label' medical conditions. This was the fourth time they were fined that decade.

Looking further afield

Big pharma is not nearly the only sector of business that appears to have lost its way. The structures that have been put in place to support business actually drive businesses to behave in dysfunctional ways. In *The Corporation*, Joel Bakan explains how corporations are given rights to be treated like you and me, like people. On the surface that might make sense, but what happens is that corporations often end up manifesting the least attractive traits of people. Corporations act in many ways like psychopaths.

Current structures drive corporations to focus strongly, sometimes exclusively, on the demands of the board and shareholders, and on the survival of the business. If I belonged to a corporation and made a decision that went against that bias, well, I would be looking for a new job. Businesses are built to focus on short-term goals, the next quarter's profits, grabbing a greater slice of market share, or even just making payroll, rather than focusing on the greater good of the community or the consumers of their products.

Banks, those places we have trusted with our money for years, are as well showing chinks in their armour and behaving like the corporations they are. I'm pretty sure I don't need to point you to the housing crisis of 2008 and the scams that caused it, or the current approach in the U.S. to continue to print money to try to keep the economy going. Those on Wall Street continue to get their fat bonuses, while the person on the street struggles more and more to make ends meet. Even though our Canadian banking system is currently in better shape, there is no avoiding the influence from our largest trading partner.

Sure, there are some shining examples of corporations or banking institutions that support the community and appear to live up to their stated vision of making the world a better place, but they stand out because they are so rare.

Government appears to be challenged in a similar fashion, for the same reasons. For countries as large geographically as Canada or with a population as large as the United States, there are too many particular interests at heart, too many regions to represent with a common philosophy for governing them. Instead, structures such as the party system compel politicians to abide by party lines rather than truly represent their constituencies, and the election cycle is so short that most politicians are focused on doing what they can to win their next election, rather than tackling the deep challenges that can make for long-term viability of the population they represent.

Are we losing community?

What is the bottom line in all this?

These various structures and industries were put in place years ago to support more homogeneous societies in smaller numbers. Over the years, though, we are seeing deep structural challenges that distract these institutions from their intended purpose. Governments can't support their wider and more diverse constituency base. The health care system is bursting at the seams and suffering from a strong bout of arrogance. Corporations by design are in the game primarily for themselves.

I don't like sounding like one of those old timers on a rocking chair, whining about kids these days, that the world just isn't what it used to be. But what has changed?

In the past century, the number of people living in rural areas has decreased from 75% to below 15% today. In the mid-twentieth century, communities were smaller, and for many young adults, there was a strong motivation to give back to that community. This might have been a period when we served on the school board or the town council, or even coached little-league baseball or ran for government. There was a stronger sense of neighbourhood, and an interest not only in our own well-being, but in the well-being of those around us.

Most people today live in the anonymity of big cities. There are still people who give back to the community, but a smaller percentage than in the past. While I have done some volunteer work over the years with different agencies, I have also declined to tackle numerous opportunities because I 'didn't have the time'.

We make the time for the things we are genuinely interested in. Most of us, most of the time, strongly direct our efforts toward our own self-interest rather than that of the common good, just like those governments and corporations out there. We as individuals, like the governments and corporations, are all losing the connections that drive our interests in others.

In the best of times, we can behave in a way that supports our own self-interest while simultaneously ensuring that the needs of others around us are met. With the intensifying pressures of the world we talked about in the previous chapter, we are all succumbing to stress and losing sensitivity to the community around us, just as that community is showing signs of losing interest in our well-being.

Reflections

What examples of reduced service have you seen from what were once 'trusted institutions'? Have you seen examples of corporations or governments being more attentive to their own needs than the needs of those they should be supporting?

Does money make the world go 'round, or is it the root of all evil?

we ignore in others the very depth that defines us

Dealing With Others

What It's Like – Everlast, 1998

The pressures of the world around us are growing, while our supporting infrastructure is starting to crumble. Information is coming at us faster than ever, and we feel we must do more things in less time.

It is becoming a busier world. Part of this is simply the additional responsibility we all face as we grow in our lives, but a big part comes from the ever-increasing pace of change. With all this pressure, all this change, the way we interact with each other is changing, and not for the better. We rarely take the time to genuinely understand one another, we're so busy trying to get things done.

We simplify to make sense

We build mechanisms to manage the huge amount of information that hits us; we simplify and compartmentalize our world so that it makes sense for us: he's a Liberal, she's from the sales department, they're a bunch of winos. If we put people in boxes, they become easier to handle and we can use a sort of stock photo to quickly decide how we will deal with them.

Unfortunately, this approach prevents us from really understanding one another and appreciating the differences among us as strengths. Instead, we see differences as opportunities to label others as 'not like us'. More than ever, we have become an us-versus-them society, regressing back to our tribal days.

Quite often, these categories we have made up in our minds, these compartments, are collections of people who have been marginalized by society in general. The outcast, the downtrodden, those who have already been betrayed by the crumbling support systems I talked about earlier. It may be the native groups who are struggling to deal with massive unemployment and social problems, or people panhandling on the street for their next meal, or the battered women struggling to regain a foothold in a shelter somewhere.

We've learned to walk past them, avert our eyes, feign a call on our cell phones, or quickly wave them off as they try to wash our windshields for spare change at the intersection. They are seen as a nuisance, a blight on society. We find ways to sweep them under the rug, move them to sectors of the city that we tend to avoid. We don't know them, we don't want to see them. We're busy getting things done, we have places to go and people to see. No time.

This is really just an extreme example of how we deal with most people around us these days. At worst we find ways to ignore them, at best we have a brief transaction and move on as soon as we've gained what we are after.

We're all deeply immersed in our own lives. We live it all the time, it's ours. Beyond what we have to do, we've got all kinds of other issues that are affecting how we see things, a huge backstory, baggage we carry with us that colours our viewpoint. This backstory has made us who we are, and has taken us to this point in our lives. If people don't know our backstory, the backstory that most of us generally don't publicize, we would probably say they don't really know us.

It should be no big leap to realize that everyone around us lives in a world just as crazy and complex as ours, and their individual stories are driving how they face their world. If we take the time to really understand each other, we have the opportunity to see a different picture. We get to learn one another's story.

Everybody's got a story

After my sister committed suicide, part of my dealing with the aftermath compelled me to take some time to volunteer with the local Crisis Centre. Over a couple of years I visited high schools and led frank discussions about suicide, which is one of the leading causes of death for high-school aged students, and about approaches for building resilience.

The Crisis Centre works almost entirely on a volunteer basis to provide support for people in need. The organization has demonstrated an ability to make a difference in many people's lives, and one of the reasons for its success is its deep commitment to the consistent deployment of its message. It does this through a very effective training program before it allows volunteers to interact with the public.

In one of my early training sessions, we went through an exercise where the goal was to help us feel the swirling madness that surrounds many of us – in this case, the madness as seen from the perspective of a high school student. In that group, I was easily the furthest from my high school years, so I volunteered to take the seat in what I thought would be a nice, cute simulation. All I had to do was sit there during the exercise.

Others in this exercise had the task of playing the roles of people around me. Some played the parts of my parents, some my teachers, and still others were my buddies in school and people from the community.

I quickly learned that this was not so simple a simulation. As people swept in with their conflicting expectations of me, I could easily feel the growing tension. My parents were on my case about my grades, my teachers were all throwing huge assignments at me, apparently oblivious that other teachers were doing the same. At the same time, my friends were swinging by to gossip about that new girl at school, or get me to skip English class to go to Starbucks, or go to the party coming up this Friday night because there was going to be plenty of alcohol there.

It didn't take long for a bead of sweat to form on my brow, for me to feel my heart rate go up. I genuinely felt the stress rising, even though I knew this was just a simulation, and no one around me was bullying me or trying to drag me down. I struggled to find a way to serve the very different needs of the people around me, and I'm sure my actions looked a lot like they came from, well, a confused teenager.

I reacted just like the confused teenagers that we raise today. Unfortunately, we merely dismiss their behaviours as hormonal, hoping they will come around and grow up as soon as possible. I guess that is what I would characterize as my 'teenager box', something I catch myself using too often with two of the people who are closest to me. After all, we're too busy with our own lives to appreciate their stories.

This work with the Crisis Centre helped me understand that complexity we are all dealing with all the time. I could see it in the faces of the teenagers I dealt with in the workshops, even if I still struggle to recognize the same thing in my own children, particularly when they seem reluctant to comply with the demands I have placed on them.

Tech can't replace talk

Unfortunately, the world is providing more ways for us to focus on our own universe, rather than understand and appreciate those around us.

Next time you are in a crowded restaurant, look around. You will find at least one group, likely more, where everyone at the table is busy gazing down at their smartphones, either checking email or texting someone. Physically they are side by side, but mentally they couldn't be further away from one another. At almost every meeting at work, you'll find someone texting under the table. At almost every intersection, you will see drivers looking down into their laps, not noticing the light change. Do they really think they are hiding what they're doing?

We give our kids iPads as a distraction when we bring them out to restaurants, or drop a DVD into the player when we head out on a road trip. We are teaching kids at the earliest age that it is okay to be disconnected, to be in your own world, to be mentally elsewhere even if you are physically present. Although reading books could also be considered a form of disconnect, we don't usually want our children to be reading at the family dinner table, or while visiting Grandpa in the hospital, or in any situations where socializing is clearly the expected activity. And it's a safe bet it isn't Charles Dickens the kids are engaged with when we see the iPads in their hands at restaurants.

There are plenty of arguments for the values of technology today. Texting and blogging has given a voice to many people who would otherwise find it difficult to communicate, allowing them to be heard. The Internet is a great source of information (even though it often needs to be taken with a grain of salt), and Facebook enables friends and families separated by thousands of miles to stay at least somewhat connected.

Technology, though, should be thought of as a way of augmenting how we interact, not as a replacement for face-to-face contact. Those 367 friends on Facebook aren't really your friends if you have never met them.

Research was done back in the early 1970s that studied how information was conveyed in a face-to-face conversation. The study found that 55% of the information came from visual cues – posture and facial expressions, for example. 38% came from auditory cues like inflection or tone of voice, and only 7% came from the actual words being used.

Think about that for a moment. As we go from talking to one another across the table to talking on the phone, we've lost more than half of the nuances of the conversation. When we drop it down to an email or document, or worse yet, a text message or Tweet (with a language all their own), it's as though we are trying to breathe through a tiny straw.

We have all experienced some email we sent being interpreted the wrong way, and more than once I have regretted dispatching a message the moment I pressed the send-key. As the information we convey to the other party moves from face-to-face to phone to handwritten to brief electronic forms, at each step our ability to empathize diminishes dramatically.

Web rage

It's not really that different from how we interact when we're in our cars. If we are walking down a crowded sidewalk and accidentally brush against someone, we'll generally be quick to apologize, and usually get a "No problem!" in return. Put us in vehicles, though, and as soon as you fail to signal for a left turn or are slow to get moving when the light turns green, I'll be all over your case, cursing and screaming and driving like an idiot so I can get in a position to show you my middle finger.

As we increase our distance from others when we communicate, our chances of encountering Web rage grow. It might be someone simply misinterpreting a text or email, or making a callous comment in response to a post he or she didn't agree with.

On the Web or behind the wheel, we can all be assholes.

We need to continue to remind ourselves that everyone around us has just as much of a story going on in their lives as we have in ours, a story that tends to drive all of us to think of ourselves before we appreciate the needs of others.

We need to recognize how the conveniences in our lives can actually impersonalize our relationships and make it easy to succumb to road rage or Web rage. An electronic connection between people is tenuous at best.

If we take the time to genuinely connect with others, to understand where they are coming from, and to empathize with their situation, we'll find that they will be more willing to do the same, and our relationships can be much more rewarding.

If we do that with people whom we would otherwise put in those mental boxes we have constructed, there's a chance that we'll meet some fascinating characters along the way who enrich our lives.

Reflections

Recall a time when others hadn't taken the time to really understand why you felt the way you did, because they were too caught up in their own worlds. How did that make you feel?

How about a time when you failed to give someone close to you the needed attention. With the shoe on the other foot, how could you have handled that situation differently?

we sometimes become overwhelmed

Self-Inflicted Wounds

Everybody Hurts – R.E.M., 1992

Learning was easy for me all the way through high school. Homework, the few times I didn't finish it at school, was a breeze. I did nerdy stuff, like extra math and physics, and joined the chess club, primarily as a way to goof around with my buddies after a quick game. I self-identified with my ability to quickly understand things; this became a big part of who I am.

I grew up wanting to be a surgeon, surely driven by the involvement of four older sisters in the medical profession. For some reason, though, when it was time for university I chose a different path and headed off to the University of Waterloo for systems engineering. This program had a great reputation, and an extremely high bar for entry. It was my first time away from home, and probably one of the most intensive learning experiences of my life. I'm sure it is this way for most kids when they first leave the nest.

The first term was a financial eye-opener. I boarded off-campus – a room in an old house owned by a stereotypical little old lady – and most of my struggles revolved around getting through school on a very limited budget. For me, university was financed solely through scholarships and through money I had stashed away from summer jobs. I had, of course, rationalized that I needed a car. It was an old green Pinto, and naturally that car needed a stereo, which cost more than the car itself, before the ongoing repair costs started adding up.

Being off-campus, I managed to devote enough time to my studies to do pretty well, and completed the term in the top 10% of the class. The money had started to dwindle towards the end of the term, though, and after paying the low weekly rent, there were still times when it wasn't quite clear how I would finance meals for the remainder of the week. Things like this weigh heavily on one's mind, particularly when you have plenty of time alone to dwell on them.

My first co-op work term brought me back to my hometown, where I could resume a much more comfortable life crashing with my parents, and stash funds away for the next term. I learned to appreciate that I didn't have to worry about how that meal was going to arrive at the dinner table every evening.

The second term back at school was a summer term, and I lived on campus, where there was a strong tendency to ignore homework in favour of social activities. I recall a lot of parties, skipping class to go diving in Elora Gorge, challenging one another to drinking games, investing a great deal of time and energy in finding creative ways of getting into trouble. The list could easily go on, but I suspect you get the message.

I recall this as a great time in my life, and I had many friends, as long as there was beer nearby. But all of that came at a cost, and for the first time in my life, my grades began to suffer. In the end I managed to pass the term, but it was clear that the faculty had given me the benefit of the doubt for some of my courses. In the program I was in, you either passed or you repeated the entire term, not individual courses.

I went through another work term at home, then back for the third year at Waterloo. I tried the other student village on campus this time around, and didn't last a week, with the insanity going on there. Knowing it would be the end of me if I stayed, I found a couple of roommates with a townhouse close to campus, and settled in.

Comparing this situation to my first term where I was rooming in a quiet part of town with a little old lady, I found out that not all off-campus housing is the same. Our antics made the previous term seem tame, and our townhouse turned out to be the party palace for the class. I also found that campus parties aren't simply wild and funny experiences like John Belushi's mashed-potato zits in *Animal House*. What the movies don't focus on is the morning-after, where we pay for all that debauchery.

The morning after the end-of-term bash at our place stands out for me. During the party, fences had been broken and police called in, and the puddles of beer on the carpet were more numerous than usual. I was assured by many, though, that we had all had a great time.

The morning after I was sitting in a ratty old chair that is the staple of college housing. I remember being alone in the house at the time, leafing through a binder full of old *Heavy Metal* magazines. I had to brush off a couple of policemen who came by to deal with yet another neighbour's complaints. During their visit I made sure to stand in certain places so that they couldn't see the contraband that had been lifted in raids on campus earlier that term.

And my head hurt. A lot.

Facing the music

It was then that the reality of the last three months finally came to roost. I had sat in exams that term where I knew nothing about the topic I was being tested on. At about the halfway point in the term, I had thrown a couple of courses to the lions so I could salvage the rest. It had been clear for quite a while that I was not going to pass the term, that I wouldn't be getting the benefit of the doubt from the faculty a second time.

It was apparent I had lost what I self-identified with the most: my ability to quickly understand things and work my way through tough technical challenges. The sense of loss that engulfed me was horrible. A couple of Tylenol hadn't even made a dent in my hangover, but there were plenty more where they came from. I sat there in that crappy old chair, surrounded by a beer-soaked rug, and wrote a letter to my family, apologizing for what I had done. I recall that it was about a page long, and I remember crying while I wrote it.

The plan was to finish off that bottle of Tylenol, to say good-bye. I had written a suicide note.

Looking back, I probably would have just puked all that Tylenol back up, had my stomach pumped, maybe suffered a little brain damage. I clearly hadn't researched the topic adequately.

I'm not sure who initiated the intervening phone call (I think she did), but it was a friend from high school who talked me out of what I was about to do. A long conversation with her helped me understand that this was a temporary setback, and there was still a lot to live for. She kicked me in the ass big-time and snapped me out of it, and I am still here today. Not that a kick in the ass is the right way to motivate me in every situation: we were lucky there.

I have no plans to stumble into that headspace again. I know what it is like to feel the depths of despair, and I know that this was entirely a self-inflicted injury. I hadn't bothered to develop some reasonable work habits to get me through what I knew would be tough challenges at university. I allowed myself to be easily distracted by anyone around me who wanted to have fun, and I got swept away by a culture of too much substance abuse, to the point where most objective clinicians would suggest that I had an addiction or two.

With the help of a good friend, though, what I thought was the end turned out to be a minor speed bump on the road, and in hindsight, I learned a hell of a lot from the experience.

A view from the outside

It is easy from an outside perspective to see that others are doing things that aren't in their best interest. From the inside, though, we fall victim to the events of our lives and are swept along by behaviours we feel we need to do, or are forced to do, or just seem like fun. While that way of getting through the world probably won't generate a Nobel laureate or world leader, we'll find a way to muddle through our lives.

Unfortunately, some of those paths we meander around on can get us into sticky situations. We rationalize that just a little bit of this won't hurt, or we won't get caught doing that, just this once. We tend to do what we can get away with, rather than hunkering down and doing our best or the most responsible thing we can. After all, what's life if we can't have a little fun, right?

Shiny objects easily distract us, and there are more of these distractions to grab our attention than ever before. We are trapped by the allure of instant gratification, or we indulge in things to the point where we feel it is impossible to do without them. The problem seems to stem from the fact that, in the heat of the moment, we're not really the best judges to determine what the right thing to do is. Often the people around us aren't much help, and peer pressure rarely leads us down the right path.

One thing leads to another, and soon that innocent little thing we did has taken us to a point where we are in a heap of trouble. Most of us, if left to our own devices, will at some point find ourselves in one of those places we don't want to be. At some point in our life, we will find ourselves only a couple of days or a couple of bad decisions away from the point I got to back in Waterloo. Through a short series of missteps, we can easily find ourselves, as I did, contemplating ending our life.

I was lucky enough at the time to have a friend who cared for me, believed in me, and was strong enough to make me understand that the situation that felt unbearable to me was merely a stumble along the way.

Lucky for me that this friend and I connected. We were 500 miles apart at the time.

A hard lesson learned

We need to decide what we do consciously. Am I doing this because it is the best for me, or is it best for the people around me? Does it lead to something I really want in my life? Is it a temporary distraction that allows me to relax and recharge my batteries so I can then go on with my life?

Not every self-improvement decision needs to follow this rigid path. That's not what I am talking about here. What is reasonable is to start exercising choice more than we do today. Take a step in the right direction. Then another. Eventually, we develop better habits.

We also need to grow and nurture a circle of close friends whom we can lean on to help us along the way. They may simply be sounding boards who will listen to our crazy ideas so that we can clarify our thinking, companions who keep our best interests at heart and help us decide what to do, or friends who can catch us when we are falling, help us clean up our act, and get us pointed in the right direction again.

Or maybe save a life. These friends don't just magically appear when they are needed.

Reflections

Think back to a time when your actions (or your lack of action) put you in an uncomfortable position. How much time did you spend kicking yourself for that? Can you take this experience as a lesson, and use it to change the way you would do similar things in the future?

What situations are you currently avoiding taking action on? What are you doing too much of that is fun in the moment, but will cost you later?

obstacles arise when we least expect them

Anywhere, Anytime, Anyhow

Ironic – Alannis Morrisette, 1996

We've looked at a wide range of issues that can arise to knock the wind out of our sails.

Our fragile environment – changes in the world around us. It might be the shifting weather patterns, the ongoing march of technology, the complexities of access to information, or any of a dozen other things I hadn't even mentioned, such as peak oil and the challenges we face in supporting our future energy needs. Even if you don't buy into some of these concepts, or you consider them to be fear-mongering, there are plenty of other problems that can severely affect us. These sources of impact are based on the strict limits and complexities of the planet we live on and the unintended consequences of our technological advances – two genies we are unlikely to fit back into the bottle.

Failures of our institutions – those systems we may have assumed were the stable infrastructure that supported us in our lives; the cracks that seem to be developing in government and big business; an overreaching arrogance in Western medicine and the trend towards medicating away our symptoms rather than facing the root causes of what ails us; or simply the general feeling that we are losing our sense of community and the strength it brings to our lives. Whether or not we are truly losing our sense of community, we need to ask ourselves: Is the failure of big business and government to support us new, or did they really have our best interests at heart at all?

Breakdowns in our relationships – the way we deal with one another. We put people in boxes as a way of quickly deciding how to deal with them, rather than taking the time to truly understand where they are coming from and how they might enrich our lives. We are ignoring one another more than we should, and fail to appreciate that everyone around us is caught up in a similarly complex (but different) world of issues, all vying for their attention. We're definitely all complicit in this distancing ourselves from one another, as we all tend to put up facades and stay within our shells. Think, for example, of how we usually respond when someone asks us how we are doing.

Being victims of our own perceptions and bad habits – our bias for short-term pleasure despite potential negative consequences; our tendency to avoid dealing with problems and allowing them to fester until all our best options have dissolved away. Being caught up in that swirling madness that is our lives, our stress levels rise, we tend to react to situations based on our evolutionary imperatives, instead of taking a moment to thoughtfully respond to situations. We have relinquished control of our lives.

Dealing with adversity

These are four very different forces that can impact us. What compounds the challenge we face is that these forces have no interest in playing fair. They won't wait to take their turns with us and allow us to deal with each situation on its own. They won't give us any advance warning, and we are just as likely to run into one major crisis while we are still on our knees dealing with another. We're not looking at a nicely refereed boxing match here; we may find ourselves in the middle of a street brawl, being attacked on all sides at once.

The good news is, we can learn to better manage how we perceive and deal with situations, and should think of this as our greatest opportunity for building resilience. We need to take advantage of the latest evolutionary tool we have been given – our pre-frontal cortex – and learn to thoughtfully respond, rather than automatically react to the world around us.

Recognizing that we own half of all the relationships we are part of, we can take responsibility and exert a strong influence in how we interact with one another. We can take the time to appreciate and empathize with others, and will get more of the same in return. We have more control here than we often give ourselves credit for.

We need to gain a deeper understanding of what is really happening with all those institutions that we have come to trust a bit too much, and we need to become more involved in building strong communities around us. At this level we are at a balancing point: while we don't have a great deal of control over what happens with these structures (unless social activism becomes our life's calling), we do have a voice and can influence the communities we choose to be a part of. We can help build new communities that actually do have our best interests at heart.

It is true that we can't control the weather or the ongoing march of technology, although people will continue to try. Rather than simply throwing our hands up in despair over this, however, we need to look at it from a different angle. The question really shouldn't be, "Can I control these events?", but rather, "Can I get better at weathering these potential storms with minimal impact on myself?"

From that perspective, there is a lot we can do. Think about earthquakes, for example. My family lives in the Pacific Northwest, and seismologists around the world are just waiting for The Big One to hit us here. When it does, there will be widespread devastation, disruption of essential services, and potential for death and despair. There's not much we can do to prevent it from happening.

But there are things we can do to temper a big earthquake's impact on us. One of the major reasons for building codes is to ensure the structures will hold up under conditions more extreme than we deal with on a daily basis, and wooden homes built to code will hold up better than the shanty towns that are sometimes demolished in other parts of the world.

Indeed, there is one building in Vancouver that has taken preparedness a step farther. The centre of the building is a concrete core that sinks into the ground, and the habitable part of the building is actually suspended by large cables attached to the top of this core. The intent is for it to gently sway through The Big One rather than toppling to the ground. It hasn't been rigorously tested yet, but it is a great example of building for resilience. We need to somehow replicate that building's core structure within ourselves to become more resilient.

Why bother with resilience?

We will all face disappointments in our lives, events that don't go our way. We deal with the ebb and flow of events every day, and ultimately must all face the end of our lives, some of us more quickly and gracefully than others. At the same time, there are many indications that we are doing enough damage to the planet and to each other that we may soon be facing extinction as a species. The likelihood of having our lives turned upside down is real and growing.

Either way, resilience is one of the most important qualities for us to hone. The tools we collect will help us more comfortably manoeuvre the bumps of everyday life. Should we face a cataclysmic event, we will more likely be able to keep our heads when all about us are losing theirs.

Resilience is our most fundamental and essential skill for surviving and thriving in the complex world we live in. You will not find in this book a list of specific practices to apply for particular situations. There are plenty of places that will tell you how to build an earthquake kit, or where to best invest your money, what to eat to avoid high cholesterol or how to win friends and influence people. These are useful and important, to be sure, but address particular situations that may or may not arise. Pursue these specific practices as you see fit, but it is not my intent to add to the collection of information that is already available.

Another reason for not giving you a specific set of steps or tools is that you need to choose an approach that works for *you*. I might identify a few tools to consider or a few different perspectives that can help you see things in different ways, but the ultimate choice is up to you. If you craft your particular approach for being resilient, you have a greater stake in the result.

I am introducing the idea that we can actually be proactive in improving our resilience, our ability to deal with whatever the world wishes to throw at us. I will talk about the importance of really understanding who we are and what matters to us, and how to take steps, rather than thinking of this as merely an interesting read and then it's off to the next book on our list.

You can develop new behaviours, new habits, a new outlook, and a new attitude towards interacting with the world around you. They have to become a part of you, an ever evolving you. I'll help you understand what makes one tool better than another, but you will make the ultimate selection. I'll warn you now that the tools you come up with by the end of this book will not be a complete set, since one of the concepts I want to instill is that searching for more tools to add to your toolkit is a lifelong pursuit. There will always be opportunities to find new ways to cope with stress, new ideas that help us interact with others more effectively, new directions we can take to build our communities.

These tools, these skills will not make you bullet-proof. There will still be times when you grieve, when you stumble and fall, when you face setbacks and adversity. With the right skills, though, you will bend rather than break. You will see the storm brewing earlier, and you will emerge from adversity stronger than before, possibly with newfound tools that you can add to your collection.

The work isn't done when you have read the last page; it's just getting started at that point. While the tools you will learn about can allow you to bounce back from adversity, they are also effective at allowing you to do well in good times. They will support you throughout your life, and building them into habits while things are going well makes them more accessible when you really need them.

Reflections

There are plenty of reasons to suggest that the world of the future will be more challenging than the world of today. What do you see as the major signposts from your perspective?

Do you see indicators that the world of the future will be brighter? If you do, is that reason enough not to bother with all this resilience stuff?

Part II - The Context of Our Lives

Before we can look at building our resilience, we need to understand some concepts behind how we cope with this chaotic world.

We'll look at how we evolved and how our brain has been a great tool to help us survive to this point. Then we'll look at how those very mechanisms that served us in the past can actually be getting us into trouble today, as evolution simply can't keep up with the pace of change.

We'll explore how we relate with others, and learn that even though the world we live in is overwhelmingly complex, we still have the capacity to influence the outcome of our lives.

Finally, we'll explore how this affects us, looking at the mechanisms in play as we struggle against all the challenges the world is throwing at us.

These ideas will help us understand much of what we see and take for granted every day, and will provide some structure to guide us as we build up our capacity for resilience, our ability to respond to being jounced.

Evolution

Doctor My Eyes – Jackson Browne, 1972

In the previous section, we looked at a growing variety of forces that can cause us grief in our lives. We've explored these in order to raise the urgency of improving our resilience. We have a tendency to stay in our current situation, even if it's not the best for us. As author and psychotherapist Virginia Satir has said, "Familiarity is more powerful than comfort." She was referring at the time to those battered wives who tend to remain in a horrible situation rather than face the changes required to improve.

Without raising this urgency, there's not much chance that you will actually take action after reading this book. If you do take the plunge and make the changes proposed here, it will enhance your outlook and experiences in life, even if everything appears fine at the moment.

In this chapter, we'll look at our biological evolution in a little more detail than we did earlier, paying attention to how the development of our brain got us to where we are today. It turns out that laziness is wired into all of us.

Brain anatomy 101

Back in the lower part of our brain, near the spinal cord, are a couple of almond-sized clusters that most complex vertebrates have, called *amygdalae*. We've got them, dogs and cats have them, and deer and rabbits have them. They're the source of what we know as the fight-or-flight response, and have been critical in helping us evolve.

Throughout time, vertebrates lived in a world where there were many sources of danger. Sabre-toothed tigers probably thought of us as a tasty morsel, for example, and one thing that allowed us to survive was our quick reactions to these dangers.

When some kind of danger is sensed, the amygdala kicks into action. It does this automatically, without our having to think at all. It releases stress hormones and adjusts our heart rate and blood pressure. Blood is redistributed to our core, making us better prepared to fight or flee. This all happens very quickly, literally in the blink of an eye. That quick reaction is critical when we sense a large carnivorous cat behind us.

The problem is that the world around us has changed far faster than we have been able to evolve. While there are still stimuli that we must immediately react to, such as the smell of smoke, we face many different kinds of threats that don't warrant such a strong reaction. Today, if we sense *any* danger, even the price of a stock we own tanking, or missing the bus, the amygdala still kicks in to do its job. Fight or flight isn't really appropriate to handle these situations.

We humans have another part of our brain that sets us apart from lesser vertebrates. This is the *pre-frontal cortex*, which sits just behind our forehead. If the amygdala is the control centre for instantaneous reaction, the pre-frontal cortex is the control centre for thoughtful response. This is what separates us from dogs and cats and bunny rabbits. We have the capacity to stop, ponder a situation, and choose to respond in a way that is more strategic, that better fits our long-term needs.

That's the good news. The bad news is that the pesky amygdala is very powerful and instantaneous, and tends to drive us to react before we even have a chance to think. It still rules much of our lives. Our amygdalae are part of the limbic system of our brain, the system that drives, among other things, emotion and motivation. It is automatic and unconscious, and allows us to handle many tasks throughout our day without having to think about them. Can you recall all the decisions you make relating to your drive home from work? Probably not, because you probably take the same route every time.

The pre-frontal cortex, on the other hand, would kick in if we were snarled in traffic and decided we wanted to figure out a better way to get home in a reasonable time. We have the capacity to think, to solve problems when we need to.

Our brain is lazy, though. We'll lean on the limbic system as much as possible, and for most of us, it takes real effort to go beyond our first automatic response. It takes a great deal of energy to do this in our brain. The body, meanwhile, is carefully tuned to preserve energy whenever possible.

That limbic system, to manage all the mundane tasks in our lives, has developed a large number of *heuristics* that allow it to decide things in a hurry. Many of these problem-solving techniques developed in the brain thousands and thousands of years ago, and they are still around. They are the sort of thing that allows a kitten, just weeks old, to know how to hunt prey and hide or run from danger. They don't need to be taught.

It's all part of our cognition, our ability to take sensory input and transform and process it to result in some sort of reaction. When these processes work in our favour, scientists call them *cognitive heuristics*. When they don't serve us so well, because things have changed, they're called *cognitive biases*, and they get each of us into trouble, every day.

Heuristics become biases

Let's look at how these heuristics can become biases.

Imagine yourself tens of thousands of years ago foraging for food in a valley. You are wandering barefoot through the jungle, looking for fruit. Since you were a small child you have known that you share this valley with poisonous snakes whose bite is not normally deadly, but can give you quite a fever and take you out of the foraging game for a week or two, if you are not careful.

You have learned that as you are looking for fruit, you have to be aware of your surroundings, always keeping an eye out for that snake. It's long and skinny, and there are many sticks on the ground that, at a glance, could easily be mistaken for a snake. If you are sure it's a snake you see, you are better off getting out of there, even if you see some fruit you might want.

Your tribe has been living in this valley for generations, and one of the reasons you have done well is that you have developed, with experience, a pretty good sense for telling quickly if what you see out of the corner of your eye is a stick or a snake. As it's not a deadly snake, that sense has been tuned to aggressively go for the fruit, and the few mistakes you have made are redeemed by the richer harvest you get overall. You've got a well-tuned stick-snake cognitive heuristic going.

Let's say that your tribe needs to move on. There may have been a volcano, or another tribe has attacked and you have to flee. You settle into another valley, and try to continue your foraging ways.

This new valley has snakes slithering around and sticks scattered on the ground, too. These snakes, though, are much more deadly than in your home valley, even if their markings are similar. What was originally a good balance of flee vs. ignore, based on the snakes you knew, falters. With these deadly snakes, that aggressive approach that served you well in your home valley will get you in trouble here. And your tribe will indeed suffer. Even if you are careful to get the word out to everyone about these greater dangers, there will be more fatalities in the future for your tribesmen.

The heuristic that worked in your home valley was automatic and instantaneous. It required no thinking, and the resulting behaviour kicked in before any thoughtful response could even be decided on. It will take more than a briefing from your fellow tribesmen to avoid deaths, and quite some time for these automatic responses to adjust to the new situation with the deadly snakes.

Until that time, what were very effective cognitive heuristics have become deadly cognitive biases, and will work against you.

A well-understood catalogue

It turns out that scientists have catalogued over a hundred of these cognitive biases that unconsciously and adversely affect what we do and the decisions we make every day. We are each affected by some of them more than others, but none of us are immune to them all. There is actually one bias – *a bias blind-spot* – where we tend to see ourselves as less susceptible to biases than others around us.

You may have heard of psychologist and personality theorist Walter Mischel's classic experiment with children, where they are offered a choice of either having one marshmallow immediately, or two marshmallows in fifteen minutes, demonstrating a bias in some children toward instant gratification. Many kids just can't resist eating that one marshmallow right away, as they have a bias towards instant gratification.

A colleague and I demonstrated another bias with a group we were presenting to last year. The *anchoring effect* biases us to rely too heavily on one piece of information when making a judgment. As people filed into the room for the presentation, which happened to be on cognitive biases in the workplace, they were handed index cards with identification numbers: 1, 999, 2, 998, 3, 997 and so on.

Once everyone was settled in, we briefly showed the group a jar of jelly beans and asked them to guess the number of jelly beans in it and write that guess on their index card. We gathered them up and presented the results at the end of the presentation. The people with low identification numbers averaged guesses close to 175, while those with the high identification numbers averaged guesses around 650.

The identification numbers had nothing at all to do with the number of jelly beans in the jar, but people were unconsciously biased in their guess all the same. Similarly, on your way to work you may notice a number on a billboard, and that number might unconsciously bias a decision or judgment at work later that day.

Evolution is too slow for today's pace of change

We are not the rational beings we would like to think we are. We all have these cognitive biases, we all have that automatic and instantaneous limbic system, we all have those pesky amygdalae ready to pour adrenaline into our system and adjust our blood flow, causing us to react to situations at first glance.

We've also got an energy-preserving brain that would prefer to allow us to go through life on autopilot, making impulse decisions as much as possible. Evolution has served us well to this point, but now seems to be working against us. How are we going to deal with this?

We can learn to respond thoughtfully rather than allowing these old, often outdated mechanisms to retain control. This is a skill that becomes easier with practice, and we must build a habit of taking a breath and considering the situation before we make a decision about what to do.

Even before that, though, we need to learn to recognize those cognitive biases in the decisions that we make every day. Advertisers understand biases and use them to great effect to sell their products. It is not too hard to see that our biases play a big part in the purchases we make when we are buying groceries while hungry, or the crazy things we might buy while watching late-night infomercials. When our defenses are down, we are particularly susceptible to impulse decisions and the influences of these biases.

Once we understand these influences, we can then reinforce our awareness of the impact of biases, and the need to thoughtfully respond to situations around us.

There may still be situations that require an automatic, instantaneous reaction to danger, such as a car coming at us through a red light at an intersection. Trust me, even if you have finely tuned your ability to respond rather than react, that amygdala and limbic system will kick in when really needed, and there isn't much you will be able to do about it. For the rest of the time, though, we need to take conscious control of the beast.

Along with the bad news, there is some good news. These mechanisms are well understood, and with practice we all have the ability to see them at work. As we will see later in this book, we can learn how to limit the negative impact these behaviours can have on our lives.

Reflections

Spend the next few days observing the behaviours of both yourself and others, looking for signs of subconscious biases leading to bad decisions.

Did you or someone else make a decision based on totally unrelated information? Did you presume that the salesperson you found attractive was better informed than the plain-looking one?

How do these biases affect the way you look at the world?

celebrate distinctions as strength

Diversity

Everyday People – Sly & The Family Stone, 1968

Have you ever been in a strange place and felt nervous about people around you? You may have been in a marginalized part of town, or in a foreign city while on business or vacation. Either way, you probably unconsciously looked over your shoulder a bit more often, kept a tighter grip on your wallet, or told the kids to stick a bit closer.

I grew up across the river from Detroit, Michigan, at a time when there was deep racial tension between blacks and whites. There were no black kids at my school and very little integration overall, but stereotyping and schoolyard taunts existed that have come to be recognized today as extremely insensitive. As a product of my culture, my environment, and my upbringing, I was part of the racial tension that existed. I've always loved Motown music, but those few times I headed over to Detroit for a concert or a dinner, I felt and behaved as though I were immersed in a dangerous environment.

Thirty years later, working with a company in downtown St. Louis, I saw similar signs of racial prejudice. The white-collar population was predominantly white-skinned, blacks would avert their eyes as we passed on the sidewalk, and in restaurants it was always the blacks who bussed tables. One person I worked with from the area described it as "... a combination of the worst of Northern and Southern racism, where the two races don't dare work together or live in the same neighbourhood."

Oversimplifying

To make sense of all the information around us, we tend to put people in boxes rather than try to understand them. While I had no idea whether crime rates in the places I visited in Detroit were higher than in my neighbourhood, one of the labels on that box was that *it's more dangerous over there*. The threat was more perceived than real, but my resulting behaviour was the same: careful where I walked, kept up my guard, got things done quickly so I could move on. The result tended to be a diminished experience.

Racial diversity is one of many ways in which we can differ, but one that is literally and figuratively in your face. For centuries, this visible difference has been the basis for feuds, conflict, and war. As we evolved, many of these visual differences were wired into us as biases, providing an automated drive to avoid or attack that neighbouring tribe in order to survive. If we add to race a few more forms of diversity – ethnic background, culture, religion – we have many ways to identify people as different. We may be uncomfortable with them living on our street, we may not want to visit their home country, we may feel compelled to cleanse the planet of their very existence.

Ethnic cleansing is a sanitized term for the practice of displacing or killing off entire groups of people that are different in some way. While we may believe we have come a long way since the persecution of the Jews in the 1940s, there are dozens of examples in present day where similar practices exist with the goal of achieving homogeneity.

At the other end of the spectrum, many of us still harbour some discomfort with people we see as different from us. This may manifest itself as a desire to quickly end a conversation with someone we have difficulty conversing with, rushing past a homeless person with our gaze averted, or refusing to answer the door when someone comes by to discuss their religious preferences.

We're all different, in many ways

Race, religion, gender, and age are but a few types of diversity that we can quickly recognize, but there are other types to consider. Have you ever watched someone you thought you knew quite well respond to a situation, and then ask yourself, "Why the heck did he do that? What was he thinking? I would have done something entirely different!"

We've got internal differences among us as well, internal motivators that drive us all to respond differently to exactly the same situation. I'm sure you know people who are goal-oriented (those Type-A personalities); or those who are keenly interested in the well-being of others; or people who have to think things through before taking action; and there are some who are those social animals that thrive in a group setting.

I could describe dozens of other forms of diversity that identify others as different from us – where we reside in the social structure, how we raise our children, what form of music we prefer. Regardless of the form, as our lazy brains try to simplify our view of a complex world, this diversity usually tends to serve as a wedge between us and others.

Diversity

On the receiving end

My wife was born in Hong Kong. Her family emigrated to Canada when she was still an infant, and settled in the Vancouver area. When at home they retained much of their culture, and like many first generation immigrants, my wife grew up with a mix of her ancestral culture and the new culture she moved into.

By the time we met in Ottawa, my wife had embraced the Canadian culture fully, but retained some preferences and mannerisms from home. As we continue to grow with each other, there are still times that our upbringing results in surprising differences, from small things such as how spicy we can tolerate our food to more important issues such as biases around raising children. There have been no major jolts, though – for the most part, we had Canadian culture in common. She was initially surprised at my inability to use chopsticks, but that was more geographical than racial – almost everyone in Vancouver grows up wielding chopsticks, which is not the case in the rest of Canada.

When we got engaged, the cultural diversity rose up as a potential issue. My future in-laws weren't all that interested in their daughter marrying me. While I never heard the term *gwailo* directly – a derogatory term that means *foreign devil* – my wife's parents actively sought politically correct reasons for calling off the engagement. "He's got asthma," is the excuse that particularly stands out in my mind.

Prejudice and lack of understanding got in the way from both sides, of course. I wasn't fully aware of the importance of certain cultural traditions and customs, such as the tea ceremony, so in some ways I might have rightfully deserved that *gwailo* moniker.

I persevered, however, and we moved to Vancouver and got married. My own wedding was the first Chinese wedding I ever went to, and even during the ceremony I was caught off-guard by some traditions that I never fully grasped.

In the past twenty years or so, my in-laws and I have had the opportunity to better understand each other's ways. It hasn't always been smooth sailing, and at times it has taken intense conversations to get our points across. Regardless, we're able to appreciate each other and accept and respect each other's customs, and we are all the richer for our experience. I still get handed a fork from time to time in a Chinese restaurant when we are all out to dinner, and it's not clear whether the server is doing so in a supportive way, to make sure I'll be able to eat, or because it is presumed that as the sole white guy in the room I haven't got a clue.

Diversity as strength

For the most part, we've got this diversity thing all wrong. It's a safe bet that you and I are different in many ways, but that's what gives each and every one of us our uniqueness. These differences drive how we interact with the world, motivate us in the choices we make each and every day, make us the unique people we are.

Underneath all those differences, be they visible, attitudinal, or behavioural, we are all human. Every one of us has distinct hopes, fears, doubts, needs, emotions, and expectations, but we have a common core of *human-ness*. We can build on that core and celebrate diversity as strength.

It is more than merely okay that diversity exists, it's absolutely necessary that it exists. Apart from the importance of gender differences that allow us to procreate, randomize our genes, and evolve, all our forms of diversity provide different perspectives and insights that we would do well to understand and appreciate, in order to survive and thrive in this world. Diversity, the very trait that could help us deal with the challenges of life, tends instead to divide us into separate camps, to tear us apart. This is even truer today as the pace of life increases.

When we don't understand and appreciate differences, we get into trouble. Think of someone you know who dealt with a situation in a way that seems foreign to you. Maybe she didn't shed a tear at the same point in the movie as you did, or got upset about something that appeared trivial to you. Perhaps she takes way less time to decide on a course of action than you would, or simply can't bear to listen to your favourite song on the radio. If you don't truly understand her internal motivations, what it is within her that drove her to behave in the way she did, you can't make the connection between that motivation and her action.

Her action was driven by everything that has brought her to this point: her culture and experiences, her view of how the current situation developed, her current feelings. Indeed, without that knowledge of what makes her tick, you can only assess her external behaviour (which is all you see) based on what makes *you* tick, your own internal motivations. If yours are different from hers in any way – and they almost surely are – then it's no surprise that you look at what she did and scratch your head. She acted weirdly based on your standards, not hers. Truth be told, she very likely behaved in a way that fits perfectly with her view of the world.

Now let's turn that around. You behave in a way that aligns with your internal frame, a combination of your internal motivations, your experiences, your culture and religion and upbringing, even your mood at the time. Just as you might look at your friend's behaviour as odd, others might – and probably do – characterize your behaviour the same way, because they have a different internal frame and don't appreciate yours.

We often try to deal with diversity by scrubbing away the differences, trying to make the world more homogeneous. Unfortunately, if we are asked to 'not be' something that is important to us – gay, white, Hindu, a parent, whatever – that's asking us to go against our own values and diminishes our sense of self-worth.

We don't have to become the same as others and buy into exactly the same set of values, but we can appreciate where others are coming from, empathize with their viewpoint, walk in their shoes, accept that their way of looking at the world is a valid one, even if it's not the same one we have. The more we can get to the point where we can accept and appreciate all the ways we are different from one another, the better off we are. We become better equipped to get close to one another, to build a reasonable level of trust.

Some forms of diversity are readily acceptable, such as hair colour or gender, maybe even which sports team we cheer for. Other forms, such as political affiliation, traditions, or religion, can be pounded into us from an early age as being the only right perspective, making it more difficult to accept apparently conflicting perspectives. Really, to assume any of these positions as superior or correct is to be arrogant, ignorant, and prejudiced. Just break apart that word – *prejudice* – we are passing judgment before we truly understand.

Pope Francis recently asked "Who am I to judge?", a viewpoint that is historically unique from a pope. We need to open our minds and hearts. The benefits are enormous. Different perspectives, experiences, and biases all give us a more complete set of views to help us deal with a complex world. We can understand more of the nuances of our own situation and make better decisions about how to respond to those situations.

If we take the time to truly understand one another, to empathize with the viewpoints of others and appreciate differences, we can always find a kernel of values where we align – that core part of all of us that makes us humans. This becomes the basis for building a lasting, supportive, appreciative relationship.

We're better off celebrating diversity, approaching it with interest, even hunger, taking the opportunity to learn about one another, gain new perspectives to enrich our lives, become more accepting, and gain insights that enable us to find solutions to our challenges. Think of the stories of *Winnie the Pooh* and the difference between Eeyore and Tigger, for example. I appreciate the Tiggers and the Eeyores of the world for their perspectives and the vibrancy they bring to the story of our lives. Without the diversity these characters bring, these *Pooh* stories would be far less engaging.

Most important, we can grow a wide, diverse network. Having a community of others to draw on for strength, ideas and support is one of the most powerful tools we can develop to be resilient. Like any good tool, that network serves us well in good times, and when we do need it, the power of a strong community around us can prevent us from spiraling down, can support us through the tough times.

The more diverse that community is, the more enriching, exciting and resilient it is.

Reflections

Think about the people you are close to. How much do you know about their backgrounds, their cultures? Find an opportunity to get to know them better.

Are there people or groups that you avoid because they are different from you? Ask yourself if these differences should really keep you apart. If you get a chance to learn more about them, you may find new friends.

make a difference in a complicated world

Complexity

Land of Confusion – Genesis, 1986

You've probably heard of the butterfly effect, where the simple, seemingly trivial flapping of a butterfly's wings in the Amazon can contribute to the formation of a hurricane several weeks later halfway around the world.

The story has been used to illustrate a couple of important ideas: that very small actions can result in massive changes downstream, and that the world is a very complex, deeply interconnected place.

There's another story, about a man walking along a beach at low tide, a beach that is littered with starfish struggling outside of their element. As he walks along, he takes the time to pick up a stranded starfish and toss it back into the ocean. A few more steps, and he picks up one more and tosses it into the ocean.

He encounters a woman, walking in the other direction, who has been watching this behaviour for some time. The woman says, "There are millions of starfish in the ocean, you can't possibly make a difference with your efforts to toss a few of these critters back into the water."

The man pauses for a moment. Then he bends down, picks up a starfish, and sends it back to the water where it can continue to live another day. "I made a difference to that one," he says, and continues along his way.

Complex, interconnected systems

We all live in a deeply interconnected world. Even when we can see the connections between our actions and the resulting changes in the world, we're overwhelmed by the complexity. We often struggle just to get through our day, let alone make a lasting difference in our lives. We feel like riders on this roller coaster of life, captive to the changes that occur, with no access to the controls.

A scientific simulation of a complex system such as the formation of a hurricane needs to take into account thousands of precise elements if we want the result to reliably predict anything of value. Indeed, in the original simulation that gave rise to the butterfly effect, when the number .506 was used for one of the many variables instead of the more precise .506127, the outcome was dramatically different. Fortunately, we don't have to worry about scientific minutiae to be able to better understand what is going on around us.

In any system, there are some elements that have way more effect than others. You could think of there being a top-10 list of causes that have the greatest impact on the outcome we are looking at. Sure, the other things will make a difference, but we don't need the precision of meteorology or rocket science here.

In the current world, we can see some of these major connections at work. Our progress in industrialization has led to an increase in our mobility and productivity, but also in the consumption of fossil fuels. That increase in fossil fuels has led to the increase in production of greenhouse gases, and also in our more desperate measures to find more fuel. The increase in greenhouse gases is influencing climate change, and the more desperate measures for extracting raw materials have consequences of their own, such as global conflicts and environmental disasters.

The situation gets crazy complex very fast, and we don't have to continue this line of thinking too far to recognize that we can't grasp all the variables, and that we don't really have control of the situation any more. While some of those interactions were intended effects (like industrialization to improve productivity), many of the interactions in our world have been unintended side effects. These relationships often form feedback loops that can be reinforcing over time. While the outcomes of these loops may be positive, they are more often unintentionally negative. Our increasing prosperity has been driven by our consumption of fossil fuels, which in turn drives our thirst for even more fossil fuels to consume, to sustain that increasing prosperity. This is a reinforcing loop as both elements continue to drive each other forward, even if the consequences to us are devastating.

These are the only important points to know about dealing with complexity: There are *many connections and loops* in complex systems, some *intended* and some *accidental*, and they can form *reinforcing loops* with *positive* and *negative outcomes*.

Just as that butterfly was not aware that flapping his wings had such wide-ranging impact, we rarely see how our actions create a long-lasting ripple effect that spreads and grows. But we do have an impact on that complex world around us. A simple, off the cuff statement, if we don't take the time to address it, can fester and grow to destroy a relationship.

Complexity

If we intentionally behave with this interconnectedness in mind, we can constructively alter the results in our favour. We have far more access to the controls of that roller coaster than we give ourselves credit for, and while we may not have an impact on the overall starfish population, we can change the life of the ones we toss back into the ocean. That first starfish you choose to toss back into the ocean is the most important one: It is you.

A vicious cycle

After my sister died I sat down and tried to make sense of it all. I wrote down the things that I saw as the major drivers impacting her at the time: alienation, depression, antidepression meds, and obesity were among the list of maybe twenty or so ideas that popped up quickly. I started to make connections between them, and it didn't take long for a few major themes to emerge. One was the negative loop formed by Joyce's relationship with the rest of our family.

As you can imagine in a family with eight kids, some relationships will be closer than others. You can probably also imagine that over time, what was originally a family of eight siblings can theoretically evolve into eight different families, each consisting of children and loved ones and dynamics of its own. Hence, the connectedness in the original group of eight meets competition.

Joyce was the only one of us that didn't move on to develop a family of her own. She had friends and acquaintances, yes, but when she went home at night, she was always alone.

Over time, as the siblings got together a few times a year, it became more and more difficult to convince Joyce to take part. Sometimes she had valid reasons for not showing up, but there were also excuses. It got to the point where the rest of us stopped making what had become a futile effort to get her to join us.

Joyce was trapped in a downward, negative spiral of cause and effect that just continued to get worse.

There are times when all of us get trapped in negative spirals. A friend you've known for years, who's caught up in a tough situation you're unaware of, says something to you that pisses you off. You react with words that might be less than kind, and that cycle is off to the races. You can be caught in this loop for years, each waiting for the other side to apologize before you're ready to move on.

The problem with this is that if you are holding firm in your position, expecting the other person to capitulate before you can move on, you are trapped in that spiral and depending on something that you have very little control over.

Instead, you can recognize that the only way out of a spiral like this is to break the endless negative loop, and that you have the most control and influence over your own behaviours. You need to take that initiative and change things, whether to recover the original relationship you had, or for your own well-being so that you can move on with your life.

Break the negative loops

I've had more than one job where I left in a huff, no longer willing to put up with my boss. In one case, I was furious with the sort of conduct I was dealing with, and I carried this anger with me for years afterwards.

About a year ago, I decided it was time to get past this resentment, and I asked the former boss with whom I'd had difficulties out for lunch. As we sat down he admitted that he was a bit surprised by my invitation. Over lunch we got caught up on what we had done in the intervening years, and the conversation was surprisingly pleasant.

Afterwards, we parted ways again, but amicably. I don't harbour any illusions that I'll ever work with him again, as he still carries some of the traits that made it a challenge to work with him in the past, but I've learned that I don't need to own all that crap that tore us apart. I have comfortably let the baggage go, and we can coexist in the universe again.

I've been able to move on. You can't change the past, everything that's happened is just water under the bridge. As they teach you in business school, what happened previously can inform, but shouldn't be the driver for your current behaviour or attitude. We need to look at the value of our relationships from this point forward, to influence actions we can take *today* to achieve the outcome we are looking for.

Which makes me wonder about the loop of increasing alienation between Joyce, me, and the rest of our siblings. If we had just had a little more resolve to try to connect with her, would that have changed the outcome at all? How should that affect the relationships with my other siblings today?

Impacting our world

There were several other major loops that affected Joyce. Hers was not a simple, cut-and-dried world. None of ours are. Looking at her situation as an interconnected system clarified quickly for me how she could have easily come to the conclusion that her only way out was to end her own life.

The reason it was fairly easy for me to understand this after the fact was that I was on the outside looking in at her situation – at the big picture. While we can try to build up an understanding of our own world of cause and effect, we quickly get mired down in our own biases and perspectives; we simply can't objectively see that big picture. And because of this, if we really want to understand what's going on in our world, how our actions and reactions are affecting the evolving outcomes that then affect future actions, we are best served to enlist the help of others. We can learn to talk these issues through with others, as they will have the objective viewpoint we can't possibly have. As they help us understand what's going on with our world, we can do the same for them, creating one of those positive reinforcing loops that we should be building in our lives.

Appreciate the world around you as a big, complex system of relationships, even if you don't need to know every little nuance of those connections. There are key elements influencing each of our lives, some working in our favour, some working against us. Use this insight to be more intentional in tackling the world. Rather than thinking that you can't have an impact, learn to exercise the power of choice. We can have a huge impact on our own systems, our overwhelming, complex lives.

Don't sit passively and let that complex world drive your life. Recognize that taking no action can generate just as strong a result as taking an action. We are impacting the system whether we are intentional or not, whether we take action or not, so let's be active and intentional.

For those negative loops we are trapped in, look for ways to break out of that downward spiral. Look for the positive outcome that can come from your actions. If there is none, don't follow that path. Find and reinforce the positive loops by refreshing the relationships that are important to you.

That butterfly had no intention to have the impact it did, and those starfish only received another chance at life because someone consciously took action. Be sensitive to the far-reaching impact of what may appear to be minor indiscretions, and proactively take action to correct the negative loops in your life.

Reflections

Can you see some of the connections between the events and actions in your life and the reactions from others?

What are the major loops that form the system of your life? Are there positive or negative loops? How can you reinforce the positive loops and break the negative cycles you are in?

Addiction

Needle and the Damage Done – Neil Young, 1972

Hockey legend Wayne Gretzky once said that there are two motivators in the world: winning, and the fear of losing. He also noted that of the two, the fear of losing was his strongest motivator. Both of these are primal in all of us, not just in those who play hockey.

Those automatic, fast mechanisms that have evolved in us are the body's way of keeping out of danger and avoiding pain. These mechanisms were great survival tools in their time, but they just haven't kept pace with today's change.

In the same manner, using the limbic system and cognition, mechanisms have evolved to help us recognize and be attracted to pleasure.

The reaction we use to avoid pain could be described as in-your-face. The attraction to pleasure is more subtle and because of that, more insidious. Just as we had to escape from sabre-toothed tigers in the past, we were also unconsciously driven to try to procreate as much as possible. When our life expectancy was very low, having a large number of offspring was particularly helpful to ensure that our DNA survived. But the nature of what gives us pleasure, just like the nature of what threatens us, is now changing far faster than evolution could ever keep pace with.

Entire industries have done very well by making it their business to serve our subconscious desires. The entertainment industry and substances such as alcohol and tobacco give us the opportunity to experience pleasure. Casinos and lotteries are popping up everywhere. Many legitimate industries, as well as less regulated and controlled ones, exist to serve our pleasures.

New things to be addicted to are introduced to us by people who are making money in the process. Indeed, monetization of addictions has become big business. Governments get their slice, provide a token media campaign or a little slogan to suggest that you should manage your compulsions in order to avoid developing a problem, then reap the rewards of addicting more and more users, with insufficient regard for the impact on individuals' lives or on society as a whole.

This is an example of those systems that we trusted revealing their true intentions: taking advantage of our innate biases, hooking us. They are no better than the pushers in the schoolyards whom we as parents fear. The same arguments could be used for big pharma and their documented practice of luring physicians to prescribe medications off-label to mask symptoms of what can be a potentially more dangerous root cause.

A little bit of anything isn't a bad thing. The problem is, when those automatic, instantaneous mechanisms we have that deal with fear and pleasure go overboard, the result can be an addiction.

Rethinking the scope of addiction

Say the word *addiction*, and for many of us it conjures up a very powerful, negative stereotype. Addiction is normally associated with alcohol, drugs, and gambling. We often stigmatize addicts as lost souls, people living on the street who haven't showered in months, waiting in line for their next meal at a food kitchen. This is way too narrow a view of addiction.

First off, pretty well anything can be the source of addicted behaviour. Include those big three, but add to the list things like pornography, eating, television, video games, shopping, even things like exercise or work. Any substance or behaviour in excess will do the trick.

Secondly, many people around you have some form of addiction while apparently leading perfectly normal lives. You may not notice any change in or problems with their behaviour or performance, but there's a good chance you don't know the whole story of what is going on.

Thirdly, even though many of us have a cognitive bias that suggests that we aren't as susceptible to these attractions as others are, none of us are immune to them. Any of us could sooner or later get caught up in something to the degree that it could be called an addiction.

Finally, addiction isn't a hard line in the sand that we cross. It's not as if we are fine one moment, then helplessly, living-on-the-street addicted the next. Addiction is a process, and the amount that we would call too much of a behaviour or substance is not the same for everyone.

Addiction is a far more complex, nuanced beast than you might think. Did you know that in North America, your children and mine are the first generation likely to live shorter lives than their parents? It's the result of being hooked on fast food, and other poor eating habits, with a resulting increase in obesity-related diseases. Many kids today prefer to spend time in front of a video screen over playing outdoors with friends.

Defining addiction

What are the signs that we are enjoying or doing too much of a good thing?

To start, we can define addictive behaviour as anything that is preventing us from effectively dealing with the demands of our day-to-day lives. These behaviours can be driven directly by our need to seek pleasure, or be a way of trying to escape from the pain of other circumstances that may be causing us stress. Addictions are counter to our well-being, and are persistent. We'll continue to behave in an addictive fashion or take an addictive substance even when we know we are getting in trouble.

When this behaviour goes too far, we may start to show secondary signs of addiction, to the point where complete strangers can recognize them. The uncontrollable urge to support our habits leads us to rationalize our behaviours, making the situation worse. We'll steal or use the grocery money to support a drug habit, or call in sick from work, or leave the kid in the car while we spend an afternoon at the casino. We can formulate elaborate schemes to conceal our behaviours for less traditional addictions as well, such as stealing a little more Facebook or video game time, for example, rather than tackling our chores or getting back to work.

There are two major ways that addictive behaviour can get us in trouble:

The first and most obvious is that addiction can consume money and time that really should be used for other things.

The second way that addictive behaviour can harm us is that it clouds our judgment. That certainly feeds the first symptom of spending time or money where it shouldn't be spent, but bad judgment has a subtle way of affecting our behaviour and creeping into the rest of our lives as well.

Here's an example. In the early 1990s, I was involved in building a large, complex project: an air-traffic control system. Many of us at the time were under extreme pressure to get a lot of work done with a short deadline, and we were stealing time from the rest of our lives so we could put in our seventy-plus hour workweek. In many ways, we were exhibiting signs of being addicted to work.

One morning, I was in a rush to get to the job, and didn't get more than a half-kilometre from home before the car stopped running. "Damn, I'll be late today!" I said to myself as I sensed the challenges piling up. This was at a time before we had cell phones, so I got out of the car and walked a few hundred meters to use the pay phone at a gas station to call the auto club.

It was a busy day for them, so all I could really do was go back and wait in the car. About forty-five minutes later, the truck pulled up and the driver came over and asked one simple question: "You got any gas?"

As the realization dawned on me, my short and embarrassed response was, "No." The tow-truck driver simply nudged the car up the road to the gas station that I had originally called from. I filled up and was on my way.

Here I was, using my judgment every day to make important decisions on a safety-critical project, and I didn't have the presence of mind to understand that I had simply run out of gas. The idiot light on the dashboard wasn't bright enough to make it through my work-addicted brain, that same brain that was making crucial decisions on a safety-critical project.

This makes me wonder: If the managers in organizations drive this kind of obsessive work behaviour, fuelling this sort of culture to their apparent advantage, are they pushers?

Examples of addiction abound

Similarly, video games are notorious for consuming an enormous amount of time, as players try just one more time to beat that level they are on, to get that next reward. It's not just teenage boys, either. Candy Crush, which flatters you for relatively elementary performance, and finds ways to get you to actually pay for more of the same, has women over the age of twenty as its largest demographic.

Game developers understand how to trigger those internal mechanisms that drive us, to leverage those short-term reward biases, like in Mischel's marshmallow experiment, and keep us glued to the controls. Even knowing how we're being manipulated doesn't make us immune.

A friend of mine spent some time as a development director for a couple of the most prominent games available. He relates that after spending a long day at work, he would often kick back and relax by spending four, five, six hours or more playing video games. He quite clearly understands that video games can affect your judgment, as he's been there himself.

For first-person shooter games, how can one spend hours doing everything one can to kill fictitious, anonymous enemies using simple, repetitive movements, without having that lower your empathy for others? How can players walk away from that screen and not have an urge even hours later to score more points as they encounter real people?

90

I myself have played Angry Birds long enough to see big fat birds flying across my field of vision when I was engaged in a different activity. I'm sure many of us have had similar experiences. That's the clouding of judgment that comes from spending too much time on something that triggers those pleasure centres in our brain.

Advances in technology, for all the good they have brought to our lives, have produced a myriad of new distractions that we can play with until we are literally driven to distraction, until we are addicted.

These diversions can be anything that takes us away from doing what we need to do, from looking after ourselves – even something as innocent as playing too much bingo.

Watch for the signs

Like many things, it is far easier to see addictive behaviour in others than it is to see it in ourselves. Knowing this, we should be much more careful before we point fingers. Addictions creep up on us, can blindside anyone – just one more drink, just win the next level on this cool app, just one more dollar in the slot machine. It starts out innocently enough. Then, before we know it, we're behind on our mortgage payments or we've gained fifty pounds or we've lost our job.

Awareness of the challenges we face is half the battle. We know that we've got these built-in mechanisms that helped us evolve, but are less effective today. It isn't reasonable for us to try to suppress these mechanisms, or to expect government to protect us, since government often reaps the benefits of addiction.

We need to build on our awareness and work with others to catch these behaviours in the early stages, before they become overwhelming. As they are driven by unconscious mechanisms, we can't consciously think our way through them; our brain is just too smart (or too lazy) for that.

We can take pause and look at the things we do, the products we consume, and critically ask ourselves if we are going too far. We can ask ourselves if we are diverting resources that would be better spent elsewhere, and find external resources to help us.

Better yet, we can build close, trusting, supportive relationships with others so we can watch out for one another's well-being. Think of designated drivers in a wider sense, where we support our friends as they support us, watching for signs of addiction and stepping in when we see behaviours that aren't in our best interest.

A closer look at the pleasures that can become addictions will show up later in this book, as we search for tools that we can use as short-term distractions. While it can be useful to grab a drink with friends, go for a workout, play a video game, or even try your luck against the denizens of the bingo parlour as a means to recharge your batteries and maintain your resilience, make sure you don't get carried away.

Reflections

Think of what you do to fill your day, particularly the free time that you have.

Are there some behaviours you find yourself always falling back on, to the point where it can be difficult to stop, or are getting in the way of other things that you should be doing? Have you been in this situation in the past?

How does this start for you – is there a pattern? What would be the benefits of toning down some of these behaviours?

be conscious of how you react to the world

Stress

Gravity – John Mayer, 2005

It can be an interesting game while on the road to watch the expressions of other drivers. When we are behind the wheel of a car or in front of the screen of a computer, we seem to think we are more distant from others than we really are. We remove our masks. This can lead to things like road rage or Web rage, but we also tend to let down our guard, and our faces become windows into what we are really thinking. Aside from the times we notice other drivers involved in personal hygiene or belting out a song from the radio, a lot of what we see is a representation of the emotions that people are feeling.

Sadly, the majority of those faces show signs of stress. There are few smiles. More expressions range from concern to sadness or outright anger. Part of it might be that road rage thing, but there's more to it. If you encounter someone in the parking lot or grocery store who you just saw driving on the street, you'll see that the mask has gone back on. The smile is there, and if you ask them how their day is going, you'll probably get the stock reply: "Good…and you?"

You will probably respond in kind. We all tend to put on our happy face when we know we are being observed, but we don't wear it when we are driving, as it takes energy to do so, and we think of ourselves as being invisible when we're in our cars.

Watch a family of ducks swimming across a pond. On the surface, they appear to be relaxed, moving along and quacking away, life is good. Under the surface, though, their feet are paddling like crazy to keep them going where they want to go, sometimes against the current, sometimes dealing with weeds.

While comedian Dennis Miller applied the duck analogy to marriage, it seems apt for describing how we get through life in general. Most of us are dealing with a deep, complex set of issues throughout our day, and we tend to keep it to ourselves. When we look at others with their apparently happy faces, we tend to believe that we are the only ones around us who are struggling through the day.

We usually believe that we should be capable of dealing with the world, that we can handle this. That expectation drives us to put up a good front, to soldier through, doing the best we can. As we don't see the anguish of others, we don't want to burden them with what they might see as trivial issues. We seldom realize we are really all in the same boat, or more precisely, we are all in our own small, unstable boats.

Signs of stress

Stress is our reaction to the collection of events or situations that has brought us to where we are at any given moment. Changes to our *physical responses, internal conversations, emotions,* and *behaviours* are four major ways our body can tell us that stress is building. If we catch these signs early, we can thoughtfully re-spond to the situation rather than merely react to what is going on around us. If we consciously choose our responses, we can reduce our stress and be much more effective at dealing with issues in our day-to-day life.

Unfortunately, there isn't a clear, specific list of overt signs that can safely indicate we are stressed. There are subtle signs and indicators we can learn to be more sensitive to, that can give us an early warning. Watching for these signs takes practice, and is more like deciphering hieroglyphics than reading a novel.

In terms of *physical responses*, remember that amygdala that messes with our internal chemistry and blood flow at the first sign of danger? Pulling blood from our extremities will make our hands and feet cold and can cause headaches. We may get all kinds of other aches, perhaps a stomach ache or indigestion, maybe sore muscles and joints. You might be more susceptible to rashes when you are stressed. Each one of us will have our own signs.

When I was young, mood rings were popular. They sat on your finger and changed colours throughout the day. They couldn't really decipher your mood directly, they were simply thermom-eters. At the Crisis Centre workshops, we would distribute small dots made of this same mood ring material to participants. We would place these *biodots* on our hands, and after a few minutes they showed that each of us had our own base temperature – yel-low or amber was cooler than blue or violet.

We would then take some time to relax, close our eyes, and go through simple, guided meditations, perhaps focusing on our breathing or doing a conscious inventory of how each part of our body feels. Many people would find that even in the interval of five or ten minutes, the dot's change in colour would show an increase in temperature in their hands, a sign that stress levels were decreasing as more blood was being distributed to their extremities.

More importantly, though, we learned that it doesn't take much to notice the signs, if we are aware they exist and watch out for them. Only we ourselves can notice internal physical signs of stress. They are invisible to others.

We can also keep tabs of the nature of that *internal conversation* we are always carrying on with ourselves. Yes, it's true – you aren't the only one who talks to yourself. We all do. It's as if we are never alone in our travels. We are talking to ourselves in the shower, as we are driving, walking down the street, sitting bored in a meeting. We are reminding ourselves what we need to get done later in the day, noticing the expensive car driving by, or forming an opinion about that homeless person we have to step over in the street. We are providing unsolicited feedback about what we think about ourselves.

This internal voice isn't something we want to stop, but we do want to observe those internal reflections. We might be congratulating ourselves for a job well done on that work assignment or that great squash game we just finished. We might also be tearing ourselves down, however, and that's the key thing to notice. If we're telling ourselves that we're not good enough, that we're lazy or a loser, or that we can't cope, it's a pretty good sign that the stress levels are rising.

There are also a couple of external signs of stress that we can see in ourselves and we can observe in others. As noted earlier, we often wear our *emotions* on our sleeve, particularly when we're not aware that others are looking. If we are happy, sad, angry or elated, it shows on our face, in our posture, in how we interact with others. Changes in these emotions are a very strong indicator of how stressed we are feeling.

Even more obvious are our *behaviours*, our responses to the world around us. At one point we might be courteous to others as we interact with them, the next we can ignore them as we are immersed in our own world of issues and problems, or react to what they say with clenched fists and screaming. A fit of rage is one of the clearest signs of stress we can project.

No clear dividing line

For emotions and actions, there are extremes at both ends, from laughing out loud to wailing, from a joyful hug to getting into fights, and a wide range of variations in between. But for both internal and external signs, there is no clear point where we have stepped over the line into stress territory.

We all exhibit some signs of stress once in a while. Nobody's life is a bed of roses all the time. Some people tend to behave in a way that appears stressed, while others tend to generally exude good cheer. While some would lean toward diagnosing Eeyore as depressive and Tigger as manic, I see them as both going through their imaginary lives as two ends of the range of normal. In today's world, however, there's a good chance that both would be on medication. The way these characters normally behave is merely part of who they are. If either were to start behaving like the other, though, it would be a clear sign that their stress levels were on the rise.

Indeed, showing signs of stress can be important indications that we are focused and interested in what is going on around us. Even after fifteen years of public speaking, I still get butterflies in my stomach before a presentation. For me, it's a sign that I'm interested in the best outcome possible. If I got to the point where I didn't show any signs of stress before a talk, I'd probably question whether I'm really invested in the outcome.

You might experience similar signs of stress before the big game, before a test at school, before walking down the aisle at your wedding. These are all normal, expected, and perfectly fine.

Watch for the changes

With practice we can improve our ability to observe our own physical responses and internal conversations, our own emotions and behaviours, and to watch for changes – in ourselves and others. There are plenty of signs to watch for, and we can't simply draw conclusions that we are stressed out if we see one or two of the signs. What we should be watching for is a change in these signs *over time*.

We should know ourselves pretty well. If we get to the point where our body is telling us something different, our inner voice is starting to tear us down more than usual, or we're experiencing abnormal emotions or behaviours, we've got some pretty strong indicators that stress is rising. For people who are close to us, we can form a mental baseline about their emotions and behaviours, and watch for red flags.

If you find that these changes in yourself have been around for a while, you need to step back and ask yourself what is really going on here. You are more stressed than usual; that is a reaction to something in your environment. Congratulate yourself that you actually caught the signs, be they uncharacteristic outbursts of anger, a rash on your neck, persistent insomnia, or whatever. Then ask yourself why this is happening. Try to discover what is causing your stress, so you can thoughtfully respond rather than be swept away.

If there is nothing you can do, you need to learn to accept the situation, and use your skills to simply relax.

If there are things you can do for the situation, you need to make the adjustments necessary to change it. Once you have done so, you can relax. There's no real value in putting things off, which simply prevents you from relaxing for a longer period of time, and the tension will build. The earlier you can act to deal with the issue, the more responses you have at your disposal to effectively manage that stress.

As we will explore later in this book, we can build a wide range of skills to help us relax, to bring us back to our status quo quickly. These might be things like listening to or playing music, meditation, yoga or exercise, watching a movie, or going for a walk. With a range of things to choose from, we can pick the one that best fits our situation at the time so we can recharge our batteries.

If we can keep our stress at a low, manageable level, we're better equipped to deal with the things that life will throw at us. At this manageable level, stress keeps us interested and engaged in the world around us. It is when we don't manage our lives carefully that things can get out of control.

We might allow the stressors to build up too long before we try to deal with them, to the point of having ulcers or panic attacks. We might allow our behaviours to progress unchecked until we blow up at others around us, or until that internal voice talks us into a deeper depression.

It is even possible that one of those tools we can use to manage stress – such as exercise, a drink or two with friends, or indulging in a bowl of ice cream – could turn into an obsessive habit, an addiction, and suck us into a downward spiral.

More likely, a combination of things will be what conspires to take us beyond the normal levels of stress we experience daily. When our normal tools for dealing with daily issues no longer work, that's when we get in trouble.

That is when our stresses can bring us down into depression, and we can reach a breaking point.

Reflections

Watch yourself and others for signs of stress. With a little bit of practice, you can easily feel stress building within you, and the earlier you sense it, the easier it is to defuse the situation. What signs of stress do you see in yourself throughout the day?

As you see these signs in others, adjust how you interact with them to be more supportive.

Despair

Come Talk To Me – Peter Gabriel, 1992

Advances in technology over the years have led to increased overall life expectancy. We have eradicated some diseases and learned to treat and cure others to prolong our lives. We are more aware of how exercise and diet affect our well-being, even if we don't always abide by that knowledge.

On the flip side, population growth increases competition, resulting in more and more different types of substances and activities to distract us and possibly pull us into addictive behaviours. The explosion of information bombards us on a daily basis. We have never been more alone, more overwhelmed, and more stressed than we are today, even if we are living longer. It is the best of times; it is the worst of times.

As noted before, we can always expect some level of stress as we deal with the world around us. We all face crises, where we move through psychiatrist Elizabeth Kübler-Ross's five stages of grief before we feel we are on an even keel again. At times, though, the challenges may pile up and become too much for us to bear, and the depression stage becomes prominent. This might be due to a combination of bad decisions and poor judgment, unfortunate circumstances, outcomes of addictive behaviour, or masking symptoms rather than dealing with deeper root causes that continue to affect us.

Compare this to what happens with a weakened immune system. If you've been working long hours for an extended period of time, or aren't getting enough sleep or eating properly, your immune system is not as strong. You are more susceptible to colds or flu, or more likely to be injured when exerting yourself. Similarly, you could imagine having a resilience immune system. We are constantly bombarded with stressors, and most of the time we can brush them off and continue on. If that resilience system has been weakened, however, we are more susceptible to a destructive, downward spiral.

This spiral can happen very quickly with significant events, or it may be a long, slow decline over a period of years. As we descend the spiral, our ability to reason decreases, we become less open to alternatives. We may start telling ourselves that our situation is too much for us to bear, and come to the conclusion that there is only one way out of the situation. Suicide has been called a permanent solution to a temporary problem.

Suicide, either completed or attempted, is far more prevalent than most of us would like to admit. Among today's youth, only motor vehicle accidents are a more common cause of death. As people get older, the rate of death from suicide doesn't appreciably change, but other causes, such as heart attacks, stroke, and cancer, start to take a heavier toll.

There is no age group that is immune to the downward spiral and the decision to take one's own life. None of us, regardless of how great we may be feeling at the moment, is immune to the possibility of succumbing to a series of events and decisions that can take us to that dark place. All of us are just a couple of bad days away from thinking the unthinkable.

A perfect storm

Back in 2008, I had just come off the strongest quarter since I had started my own business six years earlier. I had been flying to Europe and Asia, working with big companies and being treated like a rock star, making hay while the sun shone.

But that massive effort took its toll. My body was run down, I wasn't taking care of myself the way I should, and I came down with a bout of pneumonia and laryngitis, not a good combination for someone who makes a living primarily by speaking.

While I was recovering from this, I received a call from my brother to tell me that Joyce had passed away. It was a relatively quick call, as he had other siblings to connect with, but it knocked me on my ass.

Over the following weeks, I had plenty of time to learn more about what had happened, and to process all this information. I went through all of Kübler-Ross's stages of grieving, spending quite a long time in the anger stage.

I was initially angry at Joyce for being selfish enough to end her life the way she did. She had left a diary behind that spanned quite a substantial period before her death. Reading this was not easy, but it helped me grasp what had happened and why she had taken her own life. I was able to better understand what had been going through her mind, some of the baggage she'd been carrying that had affected how she looked at relationships. I learned about her struggles with obesity, depression, and medications, some of the choices she'd made, and ultimately the downward spiral that drove her to take that final, irreversible action.

Even though I gained a deeper understanding and could better empathize with her motivation, I still couldn't agree with her conclusions. And this all came too late for me to do anything about it anyway.

After reading her diary, I had more anger than before, just pointed in other directions. I was angry with how big pharma is driven primarily by ruthless corporate greed at the expense of the safety and well-being of the consumers of their products.

I was angry with the person who had published the book Joyce had used as a guide for taking her own life, despite his disclaimers and implausible suggestions that the publication was done in the public's best interest. This led me to take a trip to the local public library, where that book sat on the shelf for anyone to read.

More understanding, less anger

I made an appointment to talk to one of the librarians about the book, in what I recognize now as full book-burning mode. I wanted the book off the shelves, and from there I was planning to talk to Amazon, maybe even make a trip to see the author himself.

This was only a couple of weeks after Joyce's death. I was still quite weak and hoarse from my illness, and the librarian first thought I was making an appointment to sell her something. I argued my case, demanding that the library be a safe place for us to bring our kids to learn the good things – things that aligned with my way of thinking.

She listened patiently, then helped me understand the library's primary mandate to provide information with a non-judgmental position. To take a book off the shelves in an age where access to information over the Web is unlimited would be a losing proposition; a library, at least, provides professionally published information that has gone through some vetting for legality and content.

That librarian also helped clarify that my presumption that kids were allowed to wander free in the library might not be so reasonable. She was shocked that I would even think this way. The library doesn't control information, they manage it, and parental oversight plays a role in that management. I was well educated that day.

I still don't believe that a book on how to commit suicide should be so readily available, but I have learned to live with that reality. I have come to learn that I need to live with big pharma and their questionable practices by making decisions that allow me to live my life outside of their influence wherever possible. I have largely moved on.

Healing conversations

There was another eye-opener for me that day at the library. In my family, as part of our grieving, I have probably been the most open and vocal about what happened with Joyce, willing to talk about it with anyone who would listen. At the library, when I explained why I was there, the librarian opened up and admitted that her life, too, has been touched by suicide, and she admired my willingness to talk about it.

During the following months, as I talked to more people over coffee or lunch about my experiences, I noticed a strong trend: Almost everyone I spoke with was either a suicide survivor, knew someone who had attempted suicide, or had a close friend with a similar experience. Almost everyone, too, was surprised that I was willing to talk about it, and expressed gratitude that I was willing to listen to their story. These discussions turned out to be less depressing than I had expected. Indeed, after a deep conversation allowed me to find or lend support where needed, the rest of my day took on a brighter perspective.

Talking with that librarian and others was a key part of helping me process what had happened, process my grief and move on. I learned that I was not alone; I learned that others had gone through similar experiences and were able to move on with their lives. I learned that the conversations and connections we have with one another are our most powerful defense against succumbing to depression and ultimately suicidal thoughts. It is too easy to get caught up with our own negative internal voice, assuming the worst about how others see us, or that we are incapable of moving on.

When you are already down, it can be difficult to reach out to people you know, or even to the trained professionals who are available to help you through tough times. I've been there, and was lucky enough to have a friend connect with me at just the right time.

To make it easier to connect when you need to, it is imperative to cultivate relationships where you can comfortably talk about how you are really doing. Learn to open up and share the issues that are whirling around in your head, and know that all of us face similar challenges at various times.

You need not be alone in your journey through this increasingly complicated life. It is your job to recruit and foster that network of support. You need to be able to sense how you are really doing inside, and appreciate that connecting with others for help might create difficult conversations, but is unlikely to drag them down to the same level as you. Despair isn't contagious like a cold, and helping out isn't as risky as helping a drowning person. I would have jumped at the chance to help my sister deal with the challenges she was facing, to cry together if needed and help her see that there are people who care for her, show her that there are reasons for continuing on. I never had that chance, never really understood she needed that, although in hindsight, I now realize that the signals were there.

We need to be sensitive to our internal compass, to be sure, and we need to remain vigilant for those around us. We can watch for changes in how people are coping, and be strong enough to connect when there is any concern. We are all in this journey together.

There are so many ways we can be knocked down in this world, situations that can put pressure on our ability to cope. If we aren't careful, any one of us could find ourselves pushed to the point where we consider taking our own life. There are plenty of stumbling blocks, and the stakes are as high as they can get. This is why we need to consciously focus on building resilience.

Reflections

Have you been touched by suicide in some way – a close friend or loved one, or your own personal situation? Reflect on how you experienced the stages of grief along the way.

Learn to be comfortable with talking about your concerns, problems, and fears with others. The journey becomes easier when we realize we don't have to do it alone.

Part III - Changing Direction

How we conduct ourselves in this big and complex world is incredibly important. In order to effectively develop a set of skills and behaviours that will allow us to lead lives resilient to being jounced, we have to lay a solid foundation.

We need to appreciate the magnitude of the task ahead as a lifelong journey, something that can't be completed in a day. This requires a strong commitment to the effort, best served by a deep understanding of your convictions.

To keep you focused on the goal, you need a clear, vibrant story about how your life will improve. You will have to accept that your starting place might be quite a distance from where you want to be.

This knowledge helps us appreciate the magnitude and shape of the journey, and will serve as a sounding board along the way to help us decide whether we are headed in the direction we desire.

consciously tackle the lifelong quest

Embrace the Journey

Where Are You Going – Dave Matthews Band, 2002

Our family took a trip to France a few years ago. We flew into Paris and rented a car for a month-long circuit of the country. While we booked some places in advance and had a list of things we didn't want to miss, we tried to stay flexible and tackle each day based on where we were, what was going on, and the family's energy level.

Some of our best experiences were the ones we hadn't booked in advance. Say we knew we wanted to get half way to Paris from where we were. We would look online, make a couple of calls, and book a place to stay for a night or two. All of these impromptu arrangements were both surprising and wonderful.

We learned that surprises along the road can be rewarding as well. We would tell our GPS roughly where we wanted to be – no more detailed than the name of the town – and tell it we wanted to avoid highways. It was the side roads we travelled that brought us our most interesting highlights. We took a quick tour of an escargot farm on the way to the caves at Lascaux, for example. We also stopped in a very small village, nothing more than a couple of buildings surrounded by farmland, not even on the map. There we found a sixteenth-generation vintner, who took the time to show us around and sample his fare while describing a business that had been in the family for centuries, something most of us could never fathom.

Sure, we saw the Louvre, took in the view from atop the Eiffel Tower, and visited Euro Disney. The best parts for me, though, were the adventures along the way that we could not have anticipated in advance. We had an overall plan and specific places and events to take in, but we also had the attitude that we would embrace whatever happened and experience everything we could while we were there. We tackled that trip with gusto.

The roller coaster of life

In life, we don't have a GPS that we can tell to avoid highways, or to help us get to our destination in the fastest way possible. We can hope as much as we want that we will have a sure, quick and uneventful path to our destination, but life never works that way.

Think back on how your life has unfolded over the past ten to twenty years. If you imagine a line moving along from left to right over that time, with the height of that line describing how happy you are with life at that point, there are few of us who would have a perfectly straight line that rises over time. We'll all have a few dips along the way, things that didn't go as planned, or major setbacks where we need to recover and regroup. Some people might even have surprising leaps along the way, winning-the-lottery types of events – a great career move you didn't see coming, or finding that perfect life partner.

Our past, on reflection, was never a sure, clean and uneventful path to our destination. We wouldn't want it to be, either, because our life can't have any of the major crests we are looking for if there aren't any dips in between. For most of us these hills and valleys weren't anticipated, they just happened to us.

If we fail to manage the future, as most of us have done with the past, there is no reason to expect that future experiences will be any straighter. There will be upcoming dips and rises, so we shouldn't be surprised when they occur. Indeed, we should anticipate that they will occur, with greater frequency than before. First, as I've already outlined, a growing number of forces are at work against us, many of them likely to intensify as time goes on. Second, none of us are getting younger – our sense of responsibility rises, then potentially diminishes as we grow older, and as we age we become more susceptible to illness and injury. In the end, we all ultimately face our demise.

Nudge that lifeline upward

Recognize the past for what it was: a bumpy ride. But also recognize you've made it this far. From here, work on consciously crafting your future. Yes, it will be bumpy, too. You can't predict which direction your life will head today; it may take a turn for the worse quickly, or something may occur that increases your happiness dramatically.

You are able to prepare mentally and take steps that will allow you to bias that line, your life, in the upward direction. You do this by setting a future to work towards, discovering and using the tools to be resilient to the changes that will occur in your life. You do this by crafting your own way of making the world what you want it to be, by being conscious of your surroundings and behaving in a way that is congruent with your desires. You need to appreciate the magnitude of that effort, and more importantly, the incredible value of the effort of getting yourself to that point where you can be resilient.

Think in advance about things that could happen that might get you into trouble along the way – the flat tires, the snowstorms of life. That's why you carry a spare tire in your car, that's why you buy auto insurance. You can do things that will protect you, make you more resilient to potential problems.

You can even take this thinking one step further. Not only can you imagine the things that could go wrong, you can set yourself up to take advantage of the things that might work in your favour. You can get better at recognizing and taking advantage of opportunities. You can be open to exploring alternatives. You can try things even if you don't know whether you will like the result. If any of them end up being fun, well, you've just made your life richer. You can envision the future you want, and take steps that will increase the chances of making that happen.

You can consciously put pressure on that timeline of yours to move it upward, rather than letting the external forces in your life drive it down. This is what being resilient is all about, how we rebound against the jounce that occurs in our lives. Resilience makes the highs soar higher, the depths more bearable. We all tend to be pretty hardy as kids, as evidenced by me bouncing back when my best friend Billy died. As we get older, we tend to become more careful, more timid, more fragile, and we need to consciously work to buck that trend.

A lifelong journey

Taking a conscious stand about where your life is headed is indeed nothing less than a quest, a lifelong journey.

When Edison was trying to invent a long-lasting incandescent light bulb, he was pursuing his own bold idea, and it's safe to say there were a few dips along the way. His team tried literally thousands of combinations of materials and thicknesses of filament just so he could light up a room for a prolonged period of time. All but the last idea failed.

For most of us, even if we have a compelling goal we truly believe in, we might give it a few tries, perhaps less than a dozen, then throw up our hands and lament that it's just not possible. But Edison didn't perfect each of his inventions on the first try, or even in the first ten tries. He was successful because of his dogged determination, his ability to take what most of us would see as a huge disappointment and regard it as a chance to learn, taking him one step closer to his destination.

Edison was on a quest. That's an attitude that we can all use to approach our lives.

If we accept our quest, we are preparing for battle against a challenging foe, almost a mythical Hydra. The foe is relentless, ruthless, audaciously complex, and in many ways unconcerned about us.

Visionary novelist William Ford Gibson once said, "The future is already here, it's just not evenly distributed." We see around the world examples of challenges at all the levels described in the first part of this book. Some of these challenges will arrive at our doorstep, others will pass us by. Regardless of what transpires, the odds are stacked against us.

The battle of our lives will rage on whether we choose to engage that foe or not. We can simply curl up and allow the world to happen to us, or we can choose to make a stand. Where we are today in our life is a result of what we have done or not done in the past, a result of how we've dealt with what the world has thrown at us.

Where we want to be in our life, and how we enjoy the journey, can be strongly influenced by how we look at the world, how we respond to the world, and how actively we engage in bending the world, influencing the outcomes in our favour.

We don't need to be shooting for world-changing inventions or becoming an astronaut, but we should have a good idea about what we want to do with our lives – a target to shoot for, a rich, vivid, compelling story that drives what we do.

We need to be realistic about where we are today, to give ourselves an idea of what has to be done before we realize our dreams, and to create the tension to help drive us forward. Having a goal and knowing where you are now allows you to take over the controls, allows you to do more than be helplessly jounced around by the roller coaster of your life. Sure, there will be times you will be pushed off course, but you will be better equipped to steer back sooner.

Life will never unfold exactly as we have planned, no matter how meticulous we might be. Having grand goals helps pull us through those dips we will experience, and helps us recognize opportunities when they occur.

If you have never considered the possibility that you can influence your future before, you will need some up-front thinking to get you rolling. That's the big-picture stuff, the foundation that drives what you choose to do in life. You need to invest the time to recognize the truths that control your life, understand where you are today, and come up with your plan.

This foundation needs to be top of mind through our lives, and it will always be evolving. After that, there will always be adjusting along the way – successes to celebrate, and setbacks to weather.

In the next few chapters, we'll go through the foundation that is critical to support your becoming more resilient, your learning to enjoy and get more out of life.

The worst thing we could do at that point, though, is to think, "Finally, I'm done with the preliminaries. I can move on to the real stuff I can use today." That's a sure-fire recipe for failure. It's better to think, "I've got a decent current understanding of my foundation, and I know it will evolve for the rest of my life."

Your life will always be a work in progress, constantly changing. Resilience is all about rolling with the punches and learning how to make the journey enjoyable.

Reflections

Draw that lifeline. Go back a reasonable distance in the past, draw a simple line from left to right that tells a story of how you have felt over time. Continue that line on beyond today. Draw what you think the future holds, to some point where you have achieved the goals you want to achieve.

Tell someone that story of your life, and learn from the experience.

Appreciate the influence you have on where that line goes after today.

Commit to the Effort

Redemption Song – Bob Marley, 1980

My father was a carpenter, and at an early age I learned a little from him about working with wood. He always had projects on the go at home, from a simple box for carrying one of his power tools, to that stagecoach I so fondly remember him building at one point.

I brought some of those skills into my adulthood and have always had an affinity for woodworking in some way. Whether a carved loon or a spinning wheel or a sturdy tripod for a telescope, the projects have provided interesting challenges, and a great distraction from life's hassles. Working with wood has become a great way for me to unwind, to focus on creating something that has utility, and to devise elegant ways to do things, given my limited supply of tools.

Most recently, I've started building musical instruments. The challenge is that, when I'm done, the piece actually has to perform well, a result different from the static beauty of a carved loon. On top of that, building instruments has brought me an opportunity to learn how to play music, something I never had a chance to do as a child.

Sometimes when I'm building a stringed instrument, I experience what I would describe as Zen moments: I become so absorbed in the process, so focused in what I'm doing, that I get lost in that moment. The world could be falling apart around me, but nothing matters other than what I am focused on.

One such instance is during the manual bending of the sides – thin pieces of hardwood that need to be soaked, steamed and gently formed into their final shape. This works only when you can connect spiritually with the wood, recognizing the right balance between heat, moisture, and pressure to get the wood to relax and take on a new shape without a struggle.

Another moment is the exacting process of the final setup: carefully shaping the bone nut and saddle that the strings sit on, to determine how playable the instrument will be. The alignment and depth of the grooves needs to be just right to make the instrument easy to play and sonically true. Going too far means you will be starting over with a new piece of bone.

It's not really important what the deepest moment of concentration might be. What's important is that each instrument gives me about a hundred hours of fabulous, focused relaxation, and is a product I can enjoy with others for years afterwards, even though there can be brief periods of tension. For me, it's a perfect example of a tool to help me refresh my batteries, sustain my resilience.

For all the joy I get out of building instruments, I've always had a chronic inability to be as deeply invested in home renovations. We live in a sixty-year old home that has its share of problems, with bits and pieces that have gone past their normal expected lives. So it is reasonable to expect that there is and will always be a list of things to be dealt with, from quick emergencies like a bathroom faucet that needs a new washer, to the bigger jobs such as a new deck or fence. Some of the jobs are a disruption for the afternoon, others take a lot more planning and often require us to bring in outside help.

Most work around the house doesn't require nearly the same finesse as building an instrument, and renovation results in a more comfortable home, but these maintenance issues have always filled me with fear and loathing. I would typically hold off until I had no more excuses, then finally dive in, hating every step of the process. Bits and pieces of the job, like finishing off a few windowsills, would linger unfinished for years. I'm just not a home renovation kind of guy, I guess. As with most things in life, if you aren't deeply committed to doing a great job, the results will suffer.

Participation and choice

About a year ago, my wife and I were sitting down with a friend and talking about how the kitchen could benefit from a refresh. We had tackled it superficially about fifteen years earlier – just a new cabinet and tile floor. I thought of that approach as a stay of execution for myself, and was glad when we decided to have someone come in and do the job while we were out of town on vacation.

This time around, I'm not sure what got into me. I started contributing to the discussion with my wife and our friend, rather than trying to change the subject. I suggested we could knock out the old built-ins and headers, install new cabinets throughout, run gas for a new stovetop, and clean up that lousy lighting and frightening electrical work in the ceiling from past renovations.

We really pushed the boundaries of what we could do. If we were to replace that aging old furnace downstairs with a newer high-efficiency model vented out the side of the house, we could de-commission the chimney, remove all the bricks, and use that empty shell around it to house a new pull-out pantry.

For someone who usually found all kinds of excuses to avoid renovation work, I was really getting into it. I suggested we should go ahead and do it. All my wife could do was look at me and wonder if I had too much to drink that evening. She finally realized I was sincere when we headed out and bought all the new cabinets for our kitchen. I had to get through a busy period of travel before I could really dive in, but in September, the project began in earnest. I had already committed to it, but commitment alone did not mean I was going to enjoy the work.

Yet there were two characteristics this time that were different from home renovations in the past:

First, my wife and I had worked together and very clearly identified what a beautiful new kitchen would mean to both of us. There were some things we both wanted, but there were also things important to one of us but not the other. We worked through all our ideas together to build a shared vision of the final product. That participation brought us both a stake in the result.

Second, when it was time to take the crowbar to the old cabinets, I had fully bought in. I wanted to get this *completed*, rather than simply *over with*. I was resigned to there being some dusty days and probably a few very nasty surprises behind the walls, but I could deal with them. I had decided to tackle this, and it was time to get started. I had exercised choice in taking on this major project.

The job went more smoothly than I'd expected. Sure, there were days where I was covered in grime, days where I absolutely ached, and times when we had to sit back and figure out how the heck we would get out of our current mess.

We managed to plan the work so we didn't have to spend a few months living out of pizza boxes, and ended up with less than a week of serious disruption, when we had to choreograph the installation of the countertop and the gas fittings with our other work. Our new kitchen has been up and running for a few months now, and while there are still a few minor touchups needed, all the major work is well behind us.

Craft a clear, personal story

My wife and I each saw a desired end result that was attractive to us, and we entered into the process with a commitment to achieving that result. We had no illusions that things would go exactly as planned, and we didn't get hung up when things went awry.

For me, it brought the process closer to how I tackle a new musical instrument. If I'm going to build a new guitar, I vividly see what the end product looks like. I'm deeply engaged in the planning, and it is my choice to go down that sometimes messy path to get there.

I am fully bought in and committed to the project, and it is that attitude that makes the process more bearable and enjoyable, and leads to a better end result. That attitude is something I never really carried into home renovation projects in the past. It is a change of mindset, from *I don't want to do this*, to *How do I do this?*

Commit to the Effort

This attitude is a critical first stage whenever we want to succeed in changing something in our lives, whether it is renovating a kitchen, quitting smoking, dropping twenty pounds, dealing with a troubled relationship, or building a stronger resilience to the curves life will throw at us.

It is vital that we clearly embrace the better future we are aiming for. We need to tell ourselves a story of that better world, even though we don't currently know how we will get there. The story has to be rich and vivid in detail, something that we can taste, and something that we can hold onto in the face of adversity.

The story might be based on getting away from current pains, such as our laboured breathing when we climb a short set of stairs, or it might be heading toward an even brighter future than we have now, such as a vision of the joy a new instrument will bring even if we're running out of room around the house to store it.

Each of us needs our own view of that better world. Google won't work here, and nobody can hand you their story. That clear, personal vision allows us to take ownership of the effort required to make that vision come to life.

A vision for building a stronger resilience begins with your own story. You might feel the need to build resilience to avoid struggles you have experienced in the past, or are experiencing now – the loss of a loved one or a personal failure, perhaps. Or you might be looking at the world as a place of growing complexity and potential menace, and feel the need to build a shelter against the storm clouds forming on the horizon. Your vision might just be a little bit of both.

A close friend of ours has faced some daunting challenges in his life. He and his brothers survived a high-seas journey to

124

narrowly escape the oppression and brutality of their childhood in Vietnam. Years later, his wife succumbed to cancer after a very long, tough battle with the disease, leaving him to raise four young children.

Through all that hardship, he has sustained a positive outlook and a vision of a future where he sees himself providing a rich countryside environment for his extended family that will draw them away from today's distractions, and will act as a catalyst that will sustain a vibrant community of friends. His actions are driven daily by this vision, and he gains immense joy in taking these steps to create the future he sees.

Once you have a compelling vision of that future, it becomes much easier to choose to head down the path to achieving that future, even if you don't know exactly what that path looks like at the moment. Without that compelling vision, it is almost impossible to truly commit to taking the steps required.

That kitchen renovation was tougher than most other renovation projects I'd tackled in the past, but in the end was way less stressful. The key difference is my intentional choice to do what was required, rather than feeling obliged to do so to save my marriage.

With a clear view of what your world would be like if you had a better ability to shrug off small things that get in your way every day, or the ability to recover quickly from major setbacks that can hit you at any time, you can intentionally choose to do what you need to do to become more resilient. You can take ownership of your own resilience project.

For that friend of ours, his overall vision may never be completed. But it doesn't have to take months or years to experience the benefits of your efforts. There will be simple steps you can take today to realize some of the results you are looking for. A slight tweak in attitude or perspective can change your viewpoint. Simply letting go of some baggage that has been dragging you down for years can have quick impact.

You will find the steps you take not only benefit you, but can also improve relationships with those around you, put you more in touch with broader communities, help you experience things in this world you have been blind to before now.

We'll work through the steps of figuring out exactly what this process looks like for you throughout the remaining chapters of this book. The first, the most critical step, though, starts with you. You need to see what these changes can do for you in the most vivid way possible, and you need to consciously craft your approach and choose to take steps to make this future a reality.

Reflections

What are some of the tasks you feel required to do in your life – the chores that you hate doing, don't want to do, and would rather ignore? There's a good chance that you are stressed while you do these tasks, and you might even do a half-baked job just to get them over with.

Reframe these tasks to see how a job done well benefits you. This will make it easier to choose to do these tasks, you will experience less stress, and the results will be better. They might be exactly the same activities you have dreaded doing before, but the different perspective and attitude will make all the difference.

search for what you truly believe in

Foster Your Convictions

Higher Love – Steve Winwood, 1986

Every one of us has a collection of ideas we hold as facts – assertions we don't question, notions we simply assume are true. We use these facts to interact with and survive in the world we live in. Imagine a world where you could never be certain how much gravitational force there will be each day as you get out of bed, or how you'd respond to the sun suddenly rising in the west tomorrow morning.

Many other concepts we hold true are based on evidence we gather as we grow up, and are often backed by what we learn in school. Some of these ideas are told to us at an early age as simply the way things are. Given everything else that is on our plate, we rarely question those things we hold true, and are rarely put in the position of questioning our beliefs. For some of them, though, the evidence has built up, through either experimentation or raised awareness or experience, to the point where we have to change our ideas about what is true.

Back in the time when people had limited technology and means of transportation, a common belief was that the world was flat, sometimes thought of as a huge disk that balanced on the back of an even larger tortoise. Eventually, enough compelling evidence was gathered to convince most people that the world was actually a giant sphere, and we need not be worried about falling off the edge if we sailed too far from our home port.

Later on, we believed the Earth was the centre of the universe, and the other planets and our sun and all the other stars up there rotated around us. Celestial mechanics challenged that idea, and over time this, too, became an idea we now chuckle about. We look back and ask, how could we have been so naïve?

Yet those ancient beliefs and many others were the foundation on which people lived. If anyone came along to rock that boat, he would often be met with strong resistance, maybe even imprisoned or put to death for his crazy ideas. A divergent set of beliefs has often been the basis of wars or crusades. People struggled with having to change, and even to live by something other than what they held as a fundamental truth. We still struggle, and it seems to be human nature that we always will. Throughout the history of humankind people have had various systems of beliefs to hold on to. Many of our strongest views are ones we actually don't have any real insight about.

It seems the more you learn about a topic, the more you see there is a possibility that what we hold as true today may not stand the test of time. Just as most of us now know Earth is not flat and not the centre of the universe, it is safe to say that we will continue to learn, and to discover new ways of looking at the world around us and better models for describing and interpreting it. In the future, we will look back at some of the ideas we hold as truths today and just shake our heads at our naiveté. This is progress.

For most of us, our beliefs have come to us without much thought or effort. In the daily bustle of life, we take little time to consider how solid they are, or test them against the evidence we see around us. If these beliefs form the foundation of all of our actions, if they colour how we perceive the situation around us, does it make sense to depend on them if they haven't been vetted? Shouldn't we invest some time to consciously foster a set of convictions that we can trust to guide us through life?

My evolving world view

I grew up in what I would call a passively Catholic family. We went to church once in a while and participated only sporadically as part of that community. I attended a Catholic grade school, replete with a nun for a principal and the strict discipline practised in such institutions in the 60s and early 70s.

While I went through the motions, I never really understood the protocols of being in church and my parents generally found it difficult to keep me in line on Sunday mornings. I'm sure that's one of the reasons why our family's attendance was irregular.

I was taught the basics of the Catholic religion in grade school, but at that age plenty of information fails to hit the intended mark. Over time, our family slipped further and further away from the church community, and we belonged in name only, not in spirit. I had never really given the transition much thought.

Later, I went through university and eventually got a degree in physics. I don't identify this as an alternative to the religion I was born in, but more as a vehicle for learning how to objectively think things through, how to question assertions and search for evidence to back them up.

My favourite course in university was astrophysics, primarily because of the professor's ability to show us how to think critically. One topic in particular stands out even thirty years later: Most of us know about quasars based on what we read in the popular press – they're the biggest and oldest objects in the universe, and we continue to find bigger and older ones all the time. Let's take a moment, though, to look at how we determine how far, how big, and how old quasars are.

There are different ways of telling how far away things are. For things that are close, we use parallax: Objects against a background appear differently from each of our eyes. That gives us depth perception, and is a direct reading; it is very accurate and clean. In astronomy, we can use telescopes on different sides of the planet as different eyes, and parallax works pretty well for objects relatively close to us, such as other planets or asteroids.

Going a bit further out, parallax doesn't work as well, but we have other tools to use. Imagine you have two candles of the same size. Light them both up at night, and you can tell that one is closer to you if it is brighter than the other one. If you can measure how much brighter it is, you can calculate how much closer it is using simple math. This works for stars as well and can be used for distances where parallax doesn't work, but depends on the assumption that you know the two stars are the same size, like the candles. We can do this by looking at the spectrum of light they emit, but it's a bit dodgier than direct measurement.

Let's take this out to quasars now. There's been a lot of work that shows our universe is expanding, and the further away something is, the faster it is moving away from us. You've heard a train roaring by and noticed that, after it passes, the sound its horn makes drops in frequency, gets lower. In the same way, as stars are moving away from us in an expanding universe, the light that hits us drops in frequency, towards the red end of the spectrum. This is the red-shift in the universe, and there are ways of telling how far away objects are, based on how far their light is shifted toward the red (how baritone that train siren is getting).

For quasars, we use a combination of this red-shift and the relative brightness of two candles. Every type of star has a telltale spectrum of light, with a few bright lines based on the different gases they are made up of. To calculate the red-shift of a star, physicists take these dominant lines and move them along the spectrum until they get a pretty close match to a local star, then calculate that shift, which gives them the distance. They then go on to calculate the size of the star as well.

The problem here is that, at least back when I was in school, those 'pretty close matches' were usually only a couple of lines in the spectrum. We ran a test in class one day with random numbers, and it's pretty easy to get them to 'match' known stars. When that match showed a huge red shift, we had 'discovered' a huge, distant quasar. The science of quasars requires several leaps of faith, but generates discoveries of quasars that continue to be bigger and further away than ever, as well as major headlines and funding.

There is a simpler, but far less sexy explanation – that these things we are attributing as being massive and distant are simply stars with a different spectrum than we are assuming. I haven't looked deeply recently, but to my knowledge nobody has ever credibly shot down this simpler explanation.

Most importantly, though, I learned there are many current beliefs in science and life we hold as true that we still don't completely understand, and possibly never will. This knowledge shouldn't stop us from continuing to search for deeper understanding.

Today, as I reflect on what I believe to be true, I find it difficult to connect to any established 'named' or 'branded' philosophies or religions. There are some common ideas and themes in many that I strongly believe in, but as a complete system, each one presents challenges to me that I have difficulty embracing.

Many religions, for example, describe a deity that oversees our actions, provides guidance that helps us discern between right and wrong, which in turn acts as a guide to how we conduct our lives. Labelled with different names around the world, there are many frames of reference that people use for this idea.

I've always struggled with the personification of something that guides our behaviour and helps us properly conduct our lives on this earth, as though we are distinct from the other life forms that inhabit this planet. Instead, I see some kind of binding mechanism, some sort of shared energy that connects everything in our world together, not just the people who subscribe to a particular faith. For me, it is this shared energy – which can be constructive or destructive in nature – that I believe we need to be sensitive to as a guide for our behaviour.

One form of evidence to support this, I suppose, is my experience with a variety of martial arts over the years. Most are hard forms, where the intent is to harm the opponent or be the victor, even if the art itself is practised in a friendly manner. *Aikido*, though, is based on mutual respect for all involved and the notion that we can connect and redirect the flow of energy of our opponent away from the person being attacked, and neutralize the situation.

I recall how one of my instructors, a small middle-aged woman, could easily handle several minutes of sustained simultaneous attacks from three or four of the biggest, most advanced students in the class. She would gracefully swirl about, redirect their momentum and send them flying back out of her space. At the end of the demonstration, she would simply adjust her glasses, perhaps straighten her hair a bit, and continue the class as though nothing had happened.

Her use of her opponents' energy to redirect their aggression was but one bit of proof I have found over the years that there is a shared energy among us that we can learn to be sensitive to and that can guide us through our lives. There are other tidbits I have observed to back this up, such as a connection I have seen between positive intentions and outcomes, and there are many other components to the 'system' of things I hold true. But my intent here is not to sell you on my convictions.

My view is not your view, and that's okay

My intent here is to point out that what I hold as true has evolved over my lifetime, and I expect my beliefs to continue to evolve as I continue to grow. This is a result of observation, investigation, introspection, and questioning my own convictions. My system of beliefs, I'm sure, is different from yours in many ways. One of my beliefs is that this difference needs to be okay. It is unfair of me to presume that my views are the absolute correct ones, or that they will even work well for you.

As I was sitting down to write this chapter, reflecting on my convictions, I found I still have a few inconsistencies to reconcile. I believe it is unreasonable for me to push my ideas onto others simply on faith, and that it would be unfair of you to try to push your ideas onto me in the same manner. That very idea, as I think about it, gives me pause, as it seems that I might be trying to impose one of my beliefs on you.

There is a real possibility that I may discover something in my life that makes me question even the deepest tenets of my faith. I have learned to be open to explore different ideas about what drives the universe, and borrow insights I find along the way to fit my world view. This, for me, is an ongoing evolution. My system of beliefs helps me decide whether or not a skill or practice I am considering to help me become more resilient will work for me, and in turn the set of tools I use for resilience helps me shore up and evolve my convictions. They work together to make me more resilient.

Have a view, allow it to evolve

There are many people who really haven't given their convictions much thought at all. For me, as for most of us, getting through the day can be consuming enough. Some people do take some structured time each day or each week to reflect, although this is often a rote procedure rather than true introspection. I prefer to take time that fits into my own schedule to ponder life, and to add a little bit of reflection into many of the things I do throughout the day.

Regardless of the approach you take, there should be a system of beliefs that works for you. It is the foundation you use to decide how you are going to behave throughout the day, how to respond to the situations you encounter. It becomes the context we use to determine the usefulness of new ideas, and it is our moral compass.

Take stock, think through and understand what it is you hold to be true – the foundation of your way of looking at and interacting with the world. This isn't a test, there's no right or wrong answer. There may be some aspects you have never really thought about, there may be some bits that don't fit so well with other bits.

Consciously build your convictions, a foundation you can believe in. Not because someone told you what to believe when you were a child, but because you have applied careful consideration and truly believe they are reasonable for you. Don't be afraid to discover areas that don't quite make sense; those are the areas you can explore to better understand, where you can perhaps make some adjustments or wholesale changes to your system. Foster your convictions, and be open to their evolving over time.

Reflections

What are the major pieces of your system of beliefs that you have never questioned? Are there alternative beliefs in the world that compete with yours? How can you reconcile those differences?

choose the kind of impact you want to have

Craft a Destination

Teach Your Children Well – Crosby, Stills, Nash & Young, 1970

I've talked about how your convictions are a useful guideline for assessing how your activities fit with who you are. Many of us take our values for granted as 'just the way it is', but they need to be seen as malleable over the course of our lives to help make sense of the world around us.

Convictions have to resonate personally, and yours will naturally vary from mine. Our values are reflected in the decisions we make daily as well as in the major turning points of our lives. Regardless of scope, be sensitive to how your values and decisions impact those around you. My values reflect how I manage my career, build my family, and interact with people around me; they support my local impact. Some people, such as world leaders, make far-reaching decisions that can affect billions of people in a far more complex world, and their convictions need to encompass that scope to support them in their decisions.

I've also talked about the importance of identifying what's in it for you before acting. As you become more resilient, when you are about to tackle a big project like a kitchen renovation or a change in behaviour, visualizing your world being a better place as a result makes it easier to buy into the idea of attempting the work, and the whole effort can actually be quite painless.

It is critical to connect what you do to your personal values and the benefits it will generate. If you don't, your life will be filled with internal conflict, and you will struggle to invest in the effort required to accomplish what you need to do. But there's another layer to add at this point. We want to understand where we want to be in the long run. We want to craft an *overall* destination for our lives.

Beyond meandering

Throughout most of my life so far, I'd never really had that overall vision of what I wanted to achieve. In high school, when it came time to apply at universities, I chose engineering even though I had always thought I wanted to get into medicine. At university, I meandered down different paths and eventually chose physics as the discipline to get my degree in – not because I wanted to be a physicist, but because that seemed to be the easiest path for me at the time.

In industry and in life, there are some key decisions and events I can identify in the rear-view mirror that brought me to where I am today, but it would be naïve to assume that this was all done consciously and intentionally, with a particular goal in mind. We can all get through life this way, and most of us do. We're born, we live, we die, and the world keeps turning around us.

In the aftermath of that perfect storm of events back in 2008, I had time on my hands to ponder what I wanted from life. After listening to what people said about Joyce in her eulogy, I asked myself what I would like people to say in my eulogy. Certainly I want people to comment about their friendships with me, how I was a nice guy and all that. I'd want my immediate family to stand up and reflect on how I contributed to their lives, helped my kids grow into adults who themselves thrived in the world.

More than that, though, I would want people to reflect on how I contributed to their lives even if they weren't close friends and family who felt an obligation to say something nice about me. I would want people to say I made a difference for them, how I left a farther-reaching, positive impression on the world.

This perspective helped me understand that I have to focus on my well-being if I want to be around long enough to have that impact. While I have no illusions about being remembered as the next Nelson Mandela, I still want more than to be dutifully remembered only by my family.

What's your impact?

In working with many small and large companies over the years, a key distinction between those that merely get by and those that really stand out is the reach of their vision. The strong companies, the ones that thrive well beyond the tenure of their founders, tend to have what authors James Collins and Jerry Porras would call a 'Big Hairy Audacious Goal', or BHAG.

If we translate this to personal terms, a BHAG is a long-term desired future, something far-reaching, well beyond what the world might be like for me when the new kitchen is done. It's a clear understanding of what you want to achieve overall with your life, the legacy people will be eager to let the world know about in your eulogy.

You may know a few individuals who always seem to have a laser focus on what they want from life. Chris Hadfield, for example, wanted to be an astronaut ever since he saw Neil Armstrong walk on the moon in 1969, and this goal drove every decision he made in his life since then. There are similar stories behind business leaders such as Elon Musk, or world-class athletes such as Venus and Serena Williams, or numerous performers and artists. Indeed, few people rise to prominence without significant effort based on focusing on a clear goal.

Most of us, though, haven't really given this much consideration, or might have played around with a few ideas – pipe dreams – without any expectations. Writer Lewis Carroll once said, "If you don't know where you are going, any road will get you there."

We all need a destination in life. That destination might not be as ambitious and focused as Chris Hadfield's or Serena Williams', but it is never too late to clarify what you are striving for in your life. That destination, that 'big hairy audacious goal', helps you decide which big projects are important and which ones are merely noise. It opens your eyes to ideas that you never would have considered if you were simply muddling through your life, and gives your life purpose and direction.

Behaving on purpose

For me, thinking about my destination has driven me to be more conscious as a husband and father. I have recognized that some of my previous reactions to daily events were less than strategic, and learned to behave in a way that helps my family grow in the long term.

Having a destination has allowed me to better understand what I want to achieve in other areas of my life as well. I had always been visually creative and loved music, but as life got busy and external demands on my time pushed harder, I had stopped drawing, and spent little time even listening to music. With a newfound respect for the need to nourish my creative side, I'm learning to play and build instruments, and I'm pretty ruthless in finding time to do so – part of finding a reasonable balance in life.

Living with an overall purpose in mind has helped me appreciate that a big part of what drives me is the view that everything I do can be an opportunity to learn. This brings richness to what otherwise might feel like mundane activities. When I run technical workshops, I'm often facilitating a topic that I have covered hundreds of times before. Even though I am supposed to be the expert on that particular topic, I appreciate that every other person in the room brings decades of life experience and plenty of complementary skills to the room, and every workshop becomes a rich learning opportunity.

Knowing that my actions align with what is strategic to me allows me to enjoy the journey a lot more. There are fewer things that I do now that feel like just a job, more things that I can really get jazzed about.

A clear overall destination has also helped me decide where my life is going. As a consultant, I find that there can be a significant ebb and flow of demand for my services, and there was a time a few years ago where there was more ebb than flow, to the point where I considered getting back into the alternate world of the nine-to-five workforce. Thinking about that situation in the context of what I want to achieve in life, though, gave me pause. With a nine-to-five job it would be tougher to focus on other priorities I am interested in, and in my line of work, there would be strong expectations to go well beyond a standard nine-to-five schedule. After years of having the freedom to choose a course of action based on my own priorities, I would be pressured to meet the huge tactical outcomes that exist in most companies. Considering these issues actually made it pretty easy to appreciate my current situation, even with all its rough edges.

Probably most important for me, though, is that having that overall destination reminds me that there's still a lot I want to achieve in my life. This goes beyond all the activities I want to knock off before I die, though creating a bucket list might be one way to consider building your own goals.

There are elements of my overall destination that are way bigger than anything I could tackle as a project and check off on a list, and I'm sure that there are some that I won't have the time to accomplish before I die. If I keep progressing towards my destination, if it serves to keep me hungry and motivated throughout my life while enjoying the journey along the way, then it has served its purpose.

That destination you express can take many forms. You may want to start your own business or invent a new product. You may want to take part in a worthy cause internationally or find ways to give back to your immediate community. It may involve leadership and global change, or simply participation locally or achieving something personally. Your destination will potentially change over time, certainly it will become more clear as you learn, and it definitely does not have to be limited to one particular idea. My destination, for example, contains aspects of family, community, and personal growth.

The business world usually suggests this destination be described in quantified terms, specific numbers to reach, targets that can be measured objectively, measures that bonuses can be based on. In life, though, it's okay and probably preferable to be more qualitative and vivid through the use of storytelling. You want your vision to be emotionally captivating, a story that can really hold your attention, a vision that compels you to jump out of bed in the morning to start your day. With a good idea of where we want to end up in our lives, we're more likely to head in that direction than to simply bounce around like a pinball, driven by the events that happen around us, or the interests of others.

One part of my destination is to become skilled enough to be able to convey emotion to others through my music. I don't see achieving this through playing to a certain number of people, or publishing a certain number of songs, or having commercial success. If I can elicit an emotional response simply through playing a piece of music to someone, that's a sign I've reached my destination. And believe me, I've got a long way to go if the emotion I am striving for is anything other than pain.

A good, strong destination is much like the goal line in a football game. Unlike a game of tag where people run around the field only with the interest of avoiding getting tagged, that goal line provides a clear direction to shoot for. The destination drives all the decisions that all the players on the field make; it puts more structure to the game.

In music, I'm interested in more than just playing the notes, I want to understand how music works to elicit that emotional response, and my learning is structured accordingly. Sure, I learn to play songs, but I also recognize how music theory and the study of structures such as scales contribute to a deeper understanding. I listen to music more critically than I have in the past, trying to understand how the players get their feeling across, make that deeper connection with what they are playing.

A few years ago, my daughter was practicing piano, and she was due to perform Beethoven's "Ode to Joy" as part of a recital. She was quite nervous and didn't feel she was ready to do a decent job. I took her aside and just asked her to summon up the best memory she had in her life so far. We talked about that event for a few minutes and tried to recall it as clearly as possible. Then it was her turn to play. She nailed it, and it's that kind of connection between emotion and music that I want to be able to reproduce.

For you, that destination will put more structure in your life, give you a target to strive for, help you choose individual moves that will get you closer to that destination. It can awaken an energy for everything you do, and help clarify that some of the things you have been up to really don't fit where you want to be. Along with a clear set of values, your overall destination sets the context for everything you choose to do in your life.

Reflections

What are the achievements you would like to check off as completed when your time is done? What is your bucket list? Include the simple events, certainly, but also add some things that are true stretches to achieve.

What else would you include as your legacy? How do you want to be remembered, what impact do you want to leave on the world?

Know Your Starting Point

Just Like Starting Over – John Lennon, 1971

We looked at the need to understand your destination – what you want to achieve and how you want to be remembered. If you do this with a rich, clear, compelling story, that destination motivates you to do what's required to achieve your goals, and guides your course of action as opportunities and temptations arise.

The destination is critical, to be sure, but just as important is truly knowing your starting point, in the same terms that make your destination so rich and compelling. You need to take inventory of where you are today.

If you described where you want to be in terms of your relationships with friends and family, start from where those relationships are today. If you described a significant milestone or achievement you want to accomplish, then today's point should reveal the steps you currently haven't taken, the skills you don't have. It's when your destination and your current situation are compared to one another that you see the gap. That gap generates a tension you feel compelled to resolve, a need to take action.

Without the destination, even if it is a simple bucket list of what you want to do before you die, you're unlikely to achieve all that much. The destination on its own, though, is merely a wish, a pipe dream. When you connect that destination with where you are today, you have a starting point from which to move forward.

This reflection on where you want to be and where you are is a critical part of staying focused. That tension created by the gap between the two keeps you moving forward.

Get real

It was Chris Hadfield's clear vision as a child of becoming an astronaut that drove every decision he made throughout his life. He was singularly focused on achieving that target and he made it by filling in the gaps that were in his way. I, too, wanted to be an astronaut when I was young, along with at times a surgeon, the prime minister, and an engineer. I actually went so far as applying to become an astronaut, and have the rejection letter to prove it.

The key difference between Hadfield and myself is that focus. By the time he had an opportunity to apply to the Canadian Space Agency, he was already an accomplished pilot and had built up a dazzling portfolio of accomplishments that clearly demonstrated that he had 'the right stuff'.

Looking back, I am embarrassed about what qualifications I put forth to support my application at the time, and it is absolutely no surprise that I received that standard-form rejection letter. I was focused on and skilled at the technology work I was involved in at the time, and demonstrated excellent results, but these skills were for jobs or tasks that weren't aimed at the ultimate goal of being an astronaut. There were huge gaps in my portfolio.

In the past few years, what started as something that I did with teams in my workshops to help them achieve strategic goals in business, has now become a personal habit that keeps me focused on what I want to achieve with my life. I take that grand, rich, colourful description of what I want to achieve, and I sit down and ask myself where I am today, in that context. How am I doing with my family? Where am I with respect to those big goals and achievements?

Even though I no longer have illusions of becoming an astronaut or a surgeon, I still want to make my mark in this world. Thinking about where I am today, I'm aware of how far I am from making that mark. I've got a good understanding of my gaps, and it's that tension that compels me to take steps to reduce those gaps.

Music has always been an important part of my life. While I'll never serenade the world from the International Space Station like Chris Hadfield did, I do have a lifelong goal to be able to express myself through music that I have created. That has driven me to learn to play stringed instruments. At this point, my fingers are getting more comfortable around the strings and fretboard, I'm starting to comprehend music in different ways, and I'm able to play some recognizable songs.

I realize that I still have quite a journey ahead of me before I can really express myself through music. Much remains to be learned about composition, and plenty more about the rudiments of playing. There are probably many other concepts I need to grasp, so many that I don't even know what I don't know at this point. I am progressing, though, and enjoying the journey. Just don't hold your breath waiting for my premiere at Carnegie Hall.

Look at your whole life

For all the effort and pleasure, music is but one part of my rich, variegated life, when looked at through the lens of complexity as I described in an earlier chapter.

I also have some key relationships in my life that can be thought of as loops in the big system I live in. Some are positive, constructive loops, and some have decayed over time; they are not as vibrant as they once were, or they might even have a caustic element about them.

As I think about relationships, I try to reinforce the positive ones, and think about what I can do to resurrect or reinforce the relationships needing work. For those that have fallen too deeply into disrepair, I try to break that negative cycle – either rekindle the relationship or cut my losses and move on.

I also think about connections between my roles in the family and my roles in the workplace. For me, these are closely related, really all part of one big system. Understanding the system I live in helps me see my lifelong goals and where I am today in a different light. It helps me appreciate that there are many elements I have control over, or can influence in my favour. Thinking about where I am, where I want to be, and what I can do about the gap is extremely empowering.

Before I started thinking and acting in this way, I was getting through life as most of us do, one year following the next with little progress. The family was growing up, we would go on vacation periodically, and our work lives had their ups and downs.

These days, though, there is a difference in my perspective: With intention, I can consciously choose actions that move me closer to where I want to be, that strongly influence the direction I move in. Some people might call that luck, but I see it as behaving in a way to make more cards fall in my favour.

Brutally honest reflection

An essential part of taking inventory is to honestly reflect on how past actions have brought you to where you are now. I'm the first to admit that not all of the decisions in my life have been the best ones, and these less than stellar choices haven't been too focused on my overall destination. There has been, in the past, a little too much meandering.

There is a very strong cause-and-effect relationship between the choices we make and the results. Often our behaviour is not a conscious choice on our part, but spur of the moment, or we feel we've been forced to react to external forces in certain ways. In most of those cases, the result we get is unlikely to be what we are looking for.

Reflecting on this cause-and-effect relationship helps you learn from your mistakes and also appreciate the positive outcomes. Celebrate your successes, even those little steps that contribute to that far-off big picture you might never achieve. Celebration, whether it is simply an internal pat on the back or going out and buying something special as a reward for a job well done, is critical reinforcement you cannot neglect. You can even celebrate learning from your mistakes as a valuable part of the growth process.

Find a balance between positive reinforcement and corrective action. None of us live perfect lives, none of us are complete screwups. Appreciate both sides of your past, and consciously reinforce the positive and learn from and adjust to the negative.

That inventory, that reflection on where you are, the world you live in, and where you want to be, needs to remain top of mind, needs to be more than a New Year's resolution you forget before holiday decorations are even down. While I do take some time at the start of each year to write down my thoughts and my intended direction for that year, I have also formed the habit of reflecting throughout the year upon what I had captured as my intent. This is done through a diary that I get to every few days, where I record my accomplishing (or failing at) an activity that was on my radar for the year.

Compare this approach to what it takes to steer a big ship. It would be pretty silly to assume you can set the direction of the ship on January 1st and expect the ship to end up where you want it on December 31st, with no course corrections or delays.

Another example is driving a car. Think of the small tweaks you need to make as you are driving, dealing with traffic conditions and stoplights and the bias in your car's steering. You have to stop for gas once in a while, and it's best to keep the car in tune rather than wait for it to simply stop running from neglect. Constant adjustments are needed to keep you on course, and most of the time you don't even get into the car until you have a clear destination in mind.

Share your vision

Consider bouncing this inventory off your close friends, of where you are and your destination. We all tend to have biases that colour our view of the world and the decisions we make, so a chat with others can be very revealing about where you believe you are and what your dreams might be.

If they are close friends, if they care about you and are interested in your well-being, they'll be able to give you good, clear feedback to help you refine your perspective. You will get a more realistic understanding of where you are today, or support and encouragement for those goals that might appear just a bit too lofty, or – more likely – a combination of the two.

Bring this into conversation on a regular basis. Rather than a formal meeting to present your progress to others for critique, find a more relaxed setting to bounce ideas off one another. Make these conversations part of your normal interaction with friends. This sure beats talking about the weather, followed by an awkward silence.

The conversation becomes a two-way street, more than someone giving up their time for your benefit. You can discuss that other person's thoughts about where they are headed as well, and give the same constructive feedback in return. You build a stronger bond as you bounce ideas and perspectives back and forth, a bond that can literally save your life if you need someone in the future.

Indeed, if you are sharing with close friends, you might have a great opportunity here to find connections in your destinations, and a chance to have a continued positive impact on each other's lives.

Connecting your goals with your starting point takes you beyond idle dreaming. You intentionally build your desired future from a good understanding of where you are, and with the support of those around you, can reinforce those important connections while you are taking action to achieve your goals.

Reflections

Think about where you are today compared to the targets you want to achieve. Are there elements of the gap that will take a lot of work? Are there steps you can take to move you closer to your end goal?

What are some simpler achievements, things you can quickly knock off your list? Which one are you going to tackle next?

Part IV - Building Resilience

There are a few ideas that you need to embrace as you start your journey to build a more resilient life.

You need to learn to be present, to be in the moment. This is an incredible tool to raise your consciousness and improve your capacity to thoughtfully respond to the world around you, rather than simply reacting to what comes up.

You need to amass a wide collection of tools. These tools are skills, activities, habits, and hobbies that we can use to remain vibrant and healthy, help you relax, and contribute to the communities you are part of.

You need to cultivate relationships throughout your life. Relationships are essential to provide support when you need it, and energizing and fulfilling when times are good. It is no accident that humans survived primarily as a social species.

Finally, with greater awareness, a broader set of constructive behaviours, and richer relationships, you'll have the ability to redirect your focus toward a more resilient life.

be the best at whatever you tackle

Develop an Ability to Be Present

Living In The Moment – Jason Mraz, 2012

It has been said that people living in the past are filled with regret, those living in the future are filled with fear, and those living in the present achieve the most with their lives.

Have you ever been playing a sport or other activity that requires all your mental attention, and found that everything just seemed to click, that whatever you did seemed to be just right? It might have been a game of bowling where the pins appeared to want to fall down, or a basketball game where you could score at will, or even a crossword puzzle where the answers simply popped into your mind.

There are different terms for being in the moment. Some call the experience being present, or being engaged, or being grounded. In the sports world, this is often called *flow*, a term used by psychologist Mihaly Csikszentmihalyi in the context of the psychology of engagement with everyday life. Flow is the ability to focus on what is currently happening, not being distracted by any of the background clutter that fills our mind.

Regardless of terminology, flow is probably the most important skill we can develop to allow ourselves to live in the present, to avoid being distracted by the baggage from the past and the concerns of the future.

Learning flow

The volunteer work I did with the Crisis Centre involved workshops with high school students, about building resilience. The key goal of the workshop was to show that we have the ability, through some relatively simple meditations, to manage the stressors that push on us throughout the day.

These meditations are based on the work of Professor John Kabat-Zinn and his teachings on *mindfulness*. In the Crisis Centre workshops, I would walk the students through a guided meditation where we simply focused on our breathing – *in… out…* – paying attention to how our breath flowed, how our shoulders rose and fell with each breath, how our stomachs would move in and out. Simply focusing on the present.

The exercises were brief, but long enough to show a difference. Before the meditation, participants had applied those small biodots to their hands, and after a few minutes of focusing on breathing and relaxing, most of them found a difference in temperature; their extremities had become warmer, an indication that their stress was falling.

Toward the end of my time with the Crisis Centre, I was in a position to observe and mentor new volunteers running the workshop. This allowed me to sit back and truly relax and focus, unworried about managing the workshop itself. I sat through two separate sessions, and had about thirty minutes of time where I could free my mind of the clutter that normally resides there.

On one such occasion, I had scheduled a game of squash right after the session. I would be playing a friend I had never come close to beating in the past. This time, however, things were different: I had one of those magical moments where everything seemed to go my way. Shots that I often struggled with were easy and I was able to move to where the ball was headed with little effort. There were at least half-a-dozen times where my opponent and I would just look at each other and wonder where the heck that shot came from. I won handily. I had found flow.

Contrast that to another game I played recently. My opponent was someone who had never beaten me before, and I had been on a winning streak over the past few weeks. Instead of taking the time to meditate, relax, and focus before the game, I had had a significant disagreement with my two teenaged kids, and the outcome of that altercation weighed heavily on my mind. In the squash court, the exact opposite to flow occurred, and I lost handily.

Squash is an extremely physical game, but my performance on any given day is primarily driven by my frame of mind as I enter the court. Many professional athletes understand this, and top performers often carefully avoid stressful situations before a big match. They take time before the game to get their head in the right space. Those thousands of grounders hit or baskets thrown before a match aren't going to dramatically improve the players' skills in these areas. Practice will, though, help them get focused on their game, get in the zone, find flow.

Beyond that, many athletes will routinely use some form of meditation to make their focus even stronger. They might spend some time mentally connecting with different parts of their body to be in tune with how they are feeling. They may use visualization techniques – watching a movie of themselves in their mind as they are hitting that home run or throwing that curling rock to stop right on the button. They know from experience this makes a difference in their performance, and they know this is a technique, like many in their sport, that can be improved with practice.

The same techniques are used by top performers in music before a concert, or public speakers before a talk. They will settle in on the task at hand, centre themselves before they take the stage. It is one of the key reasons that these people regularly provide spellbinding performances. There's a quote from Mick Jagger that I use for my own motivation: "You go out there and put yourself on the line and you make sure you're as good as you can possibly be… even if you feel terrible, you've got a cold, your back's aching and all that crap. You do it because you are putting yourself on the line and those people have paid good money to see you, and you better be bloody good."

Learning like the pros

Even when we see an amazing performance and know about an athlete's ability to meditate and calm the mind to improve focus, few of us apply it to our own lives. Yet those skills honed for highly competitive situations will usually support more mundane situations as well. What athletes, musicians, and public speakers can learn and improve with practice, so can we.

When I was first training to run these mindfulness workshops, I found it difficult to focus on my breathing, even for a couple of minutes. In a world where we are constantly bombarded with distractions from every direction, it is easy to find your mind wandering to something else. Most people experience this at first.

Don't get upset with yourself if you find your mind drifting as you try to focus on your breathing. Distractions affect everyone, and the fact that you caught your mind wandering is a critical first step, a step in the right direction. Simply be happy with noticing, and allow yourself to return focus to your breathing. With time, the mind will wander less often, and focusing becomes easier.

Soon, taking just a moment to become centred becomes a skill we can use almost anywhere, in any situation – just before we rise in the morning, or in the shower, or on the bus on the way to work (not while you're driving, please), or in the waiting room before an interview, or before we fall asleep at night. Done often enough, this centring becomes a habit that allows us to calmly face many situations in our lives.

If we break this down, what we are doing is exercising our powerful but lazy pre-frontal cortex, teaching it to exert itself in situations that would normally be driven by our more primitive but automatic amygdala. We are learning to take advantage of the part of our brain that makes us different from other animals, and to thoughtfully respond, rather than automatically react, to what the world throws at us. In sports and in life, achieving focus allows us to be more in control of our game, allows us to be more resilient.

The value of focus

You have probably been around people who face situations with a calm demeanour, and others who seem to be high-strung. You probably prefer being around those in the former category, and have noticed that how they respond or react to situations generates markedly different results.

In today's world, unfortunately, there are many distractions working against us as we try to calmly get through our day. We are being bombarded with more information than ever, even if most of it is irrelevant, and we are being asked to get more done in less time. With so much on our plate, our minds are cluttered and we lose focus.

We tend to communicate with one another abruptly, increasing the likelihood that we don't have the same understanding of what was said. Many people believe multitasking allows us to get several things done at once, but the reality is just the opposite; we become more distracted, and tend to do all those things more poorly.

With today's push to do more and the bad habits we have developed, we are actually getting less done and making more mistakes than ever before. The mistakes we make often cost us even more time, as we need to go back and clean up the mess.

If we really want to achieve more, we need to slow down, not speed up. Learning to focus is a critical skill for us to practice. We need to stop trying to do too many things at once. Rather than juggle three things at the same time, choose the order you want to do them in and tackle them one after another. No matter what you are doing, learn to focus on doing that one thing well. If you are taking a bubble bath, make it the most relaxing bubble bath you have ever had. Be in the moment. It applies to both the mundane elements of life – putting out the garbage with admirable regularity or being the best damned dishwasher the world has seen – or the more exciting aspects – taking that last shot at the basket as the buzzer goes or making closing arguments in a court case.

When someone is talking to you, take the time to listen to what they have to say, to understand what they are communicating, and ask questions for clarification if necessary. Don't allow your mind to drift over to what you need to pick up at the grocery store on the way home from work. Be the best damned listener in the world at that moment.

Focus is a universal skill

Being in the moment, able to thoughtfully respond to situations rather than reacting with our more primitive fight-or-flight reactions, provides advantages beyond improving performance. For ourselves, this allows us to behave in a manner that reflects our faith and beliefs, not straying far from our intended path. In our relationships, thoughtfully considering situations before acting allows us to ask ourselves a critical question: "What positive outcome am I looking to achieve with this behaviour?" If you have no good answer to this question, then you have an opportunity to change that behaviour.

In the next chapter, I'll talk about how to add to your set of skills: activities to stay healthy and fit; habits that will grow your mind or nourish your spirituality or help you relax; life choices to keep you vibrant and focused on achieving whatever you want in life. All these skills become much more effective, much more valuable, when you learn to be present and focused on the moment. Mindfulness is a skill we are all capable of learning with a little bit of effort and practice.

Reflections

Where are you in the range between having a calm demeanour and being high-strung? Do you tend to calmly respond to situations or quickly react? How do your actions impact you and those around you?

Take a few moments, close your eyes, sit comfortably, and simply focus on your breathing. Don't try to correct your breathing in any way, just silently observe what is happening with your body. If you find your mind wandering, simply be happy that you caught that wandering, and return your focus to your breathing. After a few moments, open your eyes. Do you notice any difference in how you feel?

find joy in a wide range of activities

Assemble a Set of Tools

Where I Go – Natalie Merchant, 1995

In the previous section, I described a framework to guide our lives: our convictions, our goals in life, and where we are now. I was careful to note that this framework is always a work in progress, a never-ending story that will change based on events and self-discovery. That framework sets the scene, giving us a far-reaching, strategic target to shoot for.

In this section we look at skills and practices to help us achieve our goals, while helping us to navigate each day of our lives. Rather than just thinking about what you are reaching for, these tools help you understand what you can do to get there.

Gather many tools

Think about the tools you have in your kitchen. You've got quite a few knives, spoons, and forks that are used by everyone, every day. You also have a few knives for preparing food, some scissors to cut things, some spatulas and flippers, maybe even a cherry pitter and a garlic press you use less frequently. There are probably a few small appliances, such as a blender and a coffee maker. Over time, you have amassed a range of tools in the kitchen that allow you to prepare and eat pretty well anything you would like, though you don't spend an excessive amount of time with some of them.

Similarly, for personal resilience, you will need to gather many different tools to be successful. These include favourite pastimes or hobbies that engage you, skills you develop to interact effectively with those about you, and perspectives that allow you to understand the world and respond to situations appropriately. Some of these tools you will use every day, as you do a fork and knife, others might be called upon far less frequently, like that salad dressing whipper you use once a year. It makes no sense to become overly dependent on any of them; they are a means to an end.

We can't possibly get through our lives with a single response to every situation that arises. If we tried, we would quickly fall into a rut. From there it becomes too easy for our inner voice to take control with negative talk about how we're not getting things done, or how we're always repeating tedious patterns, and the downward spiral will start.

About twenty-five years ago, my wife and I found ourselves in that very situation. We would go to our jobs in the morning, often work a few extra hours, then come home and turn on the TV. We would surf around until we found something to hold our interest, and take advantage of commercial breaks to slap something together for dinner or grab a quick shower. Around eleven o'clock, we would finally build up the resolve to shut off the TV, go to bed, and start the whole cycle again the next day. Sound familiar? These days the Internet has replaced TV for many people, and there are plenty of other distractions available.

One day, it occurred to us that this routine wasn't working. Sure, watching TV isn't such a bad thing in small doses, but we were going overboard. We cancelled our cable subscription, got off our butts, and started to *do* things. To start, we felt awkward, not sure what we should do with our time, but once we got rolling, we achieved far more and enjoyed the journey.

Find tools that work for you

The tools that help us get through life need to resonate, they need to jazz us. There isn't a standard set of skills and activities that I can list here in this book; you need to go out and seek them, make them your own.

In my search for activities that resonate for me, I found it helpful to see what other people love to do, and sometimes try them out for myself. My wife, for example, is fond of the fibre arts. She knits, and has migrated over to weaving, dyeing, and spinning her own raw materials. She has even suggested that we should raise our own sheep, though we haven't yet succumbed to the temptation.

With all that knitting and weaving going on, all those materials lying around the house, I thought I would give it a try. Knitting appeared to be relaxing, and useful products came out of the activity, so why not? I chose to knit myself a cardigan sweater. It didn't take long to learn the basics of casting on, the difference between a knit and a purl, and a few other things to get me going.

The project had mixed results. Given all the mistakes I made, especially the ones I found only well after I'd made them, I probably unravelled the equivalent of two whole sweaters just to finish that one. The completed product is recognizable as a sweater, but you won't see me wearing it in public.

I saw the project through, but I will never willingly pick up a pair of knitting needles again. Knitting clearly is not an activity that resonates with me. Ditto for dancing, or running on a treadmill, or a day in the shopping mall.

On the other hand, I've always been fond of music. Growing up on the doorstep of the Motown sound and having five older sisters, I was under some strong influences. Much of my childhood and early adulthood has a soundtrack, and there are many songs that fondly bring me back to those days.

Listening to tunes stopped for a while in adulthood, as a house full of music didn't resonate with my wife. When I drive the car there's music playing, but when she's driving, it's news and talk radio. A few years ago I sold off my collection of vinyl and my stereo system because they were never being used. Losing what had been a useful tool for relaxation – a pastime that I enjoyed, that never got in the way of what I needed to do – created a void in my life.

When I started to rekindle my love for music, I listened more, and this time I started learning to play, which has opened a whole new world for me. I've tied that joy in music to my interest in working with wood to build musical instruments, adding another layer of complexity to the mix. This hobby has grown into a lifetime of learning and interesting challenges, with several facets to keep me busy. Most important, though, I've learned again that music really resonates for me. I'm passionate about it, and it ties directly to one of my lifelong goals of being able to express myself to others through music.

Criteria for tool goodness

You need a variety of tools, and these tools need to resonate with you. These tools will help you stay fresh and vital, recharge your batteries, and relax. You will use them to stretch your imagination, keep you in shape, sustain your relationships, and nourish your soul.

I can't prescribe a list of tools for you. You may be very interested in knitting, and not concerned at all about music, and that's okay. What I can do, though, is give you some criteria to consider as you hunt for the right tools for yourself. There are many considerations, and there's a good chance that in your travels you will find a few more ways of deciding whether a skill or activity works for you.

Support your own health and well-being. You might be into strenuous or competitive sports (which can burn off stress chemicals, such as adrenaline), or more inclined to simply go for a walk in the park. You might need to focus on a balanced diet, and take the time to eat right more often than you do now.

Relax and unwind. Meditation works for many people, or you might prefer yoga, or curling up with a good book in front of a fire. Watching a great movie or your favourite TV show can serve the purpose as well.

Challenge yourself. There should be a few avenues you can follow that will stretch you, stimulate you to grow and learn new things. Hobbies can be great here, or a game or activity that compels you to think creatively or solve problems. You should also have some means of keeping connected to events in the world around you.

Nourish your soul. There are times when you should do things that bring an emotional response, or help you express your spirituality. This might include keeping a journal of your thoughts, feelings, and ideas; regular participation in a church community and religious observances; or more personal reflection or prayer. I would also add a need to stay connected with nature, with the world around you.

Build relationships. It is great to have a few activities you can rely on to bring you closer to others. Team sports, community work, volunteering, or projects that need a group of people to work together can be uplifting. These also serve to build relationships and in turn open up all manner of new opportunities for growth.

There are practical considerations for what you take on as tools. Activities should all be *within your limitations of time and money*. Think also about convenience and flexibility, whether you can apply these skills and activities in different situations. Diving into a good book or knitting while riding the bus home is great, but that's probably not the best place to assemble the birdhouse you're building. Look for variety and balance, and look for tools that satisfy a number of the above criteria at the same time.

You should choose activities that *align nicely with your long-term goals*. For me, exploring music is a means toward one of my goals; you might be interested in an exercise program suited toward a lifelong dream of climbing Kilimanjaro. You may find that one of your goals will point you toward certain activities, or you may find a new activity that in turn reveals a big goal to shoot for.

These tools don't all have to be habits or hobbies. A rewarding day at a spa can do wonders once in a while. Perhaps a cooking course or a trip to someplace you have always wanted to see can have a positive impact that lasts quite a long time.

There are a couple of considerations that might not rule out an activity, but you should be aware of potential concerns. Some tools can be more likely to lead to overuse and eventual addiction. It can be relaxing to spend an evening at the casino or have a glass of wine with dinner, but both can be taken too far. More of a good thing doesn't always make it better. Also, you should be less inclined to adopt activities that can cloud your judgment or interfere with tasks you need to get done.

An evolving, flexible list

There isn't a single activity that can possibly satisfy all of these considerations. As time goes on you may find that some things you are doing are getting stale, while other ideas pop up and you add new activities to the list. When I was younger, I used to skydive. These days, however, I'm a little more risk-averse.

Some of these considerations may be more important to you than others. You may have current habits that you need to break, you may need to find a way to get yourself in better physical shape.

In this long list of considerations, there were probably a few things that made you think, "Yuck, never in a million years." But there were surely a few where your thinking was more like, "Hey, I might enjoy that." Give yourself everlasting permission to try new things, to continue pushing your boundaries.

There will be some things you try that you realize aren't for you. That's good, now you know, simply move on to the next one. Experiment, learn, grow, but don't knock something until you have tried it. While I can legitimately say I don't like knitting, I don't have a valid opinion yet about playing rugby.

Armed with enough of these options, you will always be equipped with a good response to the question, "So what do I do now?" That might be how to fill some spare time, or how to recover from stress, or how to solve a particular challenge you're facing. You will have a flexible set of responses to deal with a wide set of issues, making you more resilient. That resilience makes it easier to get through the day, deal with whatever the world throws at you, and help you achieve the big goals in your life.

Overall, retain a healthy, positive hunger for stretching your limits, learning new skills, finding ways to stay energized and vital, regardless of what the world throws at you. You'll be equipped to get past any of the daily issues you face and able to recover and thrive again after major setbacks.

Reflections

What currently fills the time in your day? Do you have the variety and challenge of activities and hobbies to support a healthy, resilient life?

Are there activities you have always wanted to try that might interest you a little more now?

What activities consume too much of your time, blocking you from making time for new things?

build many rich connections

Cultivate Relationships

Lean On Me – Bill Withers, 1972

Most of our time on this planet finds us engaged in relationships of many different flavours. We interact with people as we prepare to face the day, on the way to work or school, throughout the day and well into the evening. We can easily engage with fifty people in a day. There was that driver who cut you off on the way home, the co-worker who brought your favourite coffee without asking, the kids telling you about their day or trying to talk their way out of trouble.

If we think about the quality of these relationships, we'll see a wide range. Some interactions will be relatively shallow: That person who cut you off might not have even seen you. Other connections will be deeper: the relationships we have grown and nurtured over time.

There's another relationship to consider here – the most persistent and important one we have: how we engage with ourselves. That inner voice that is with us throughout our life is subject to the same characteristics as any other relationship.

There may be times when we ignore that inner voice, times when we wish it would just go away. You may have developed quite a close and respectful association with that inner voice, or it may be the one that tears you down more than anyone else around you does. While we may try to distance ourselves from other relationships in our lives, there is no escaping that internal connection. Find a way to get along with yourself, as this relationship is often a close reflection of how you get along with others.

Relationships need constant work

There is no denying that relationships are challenging. Lifelong allegiances can gradually wither away or die in a single moment. In any relationship, there are times when the participants disagree with one another or get angry. Relationships can end as people move on in their lives, find other interests, take advantage of a great opportunity thousands of miles away, or die.

All of these scenarios bring pain and suffering. At times you might wonder why the heck we even bother to maintain connections. Some people follow that line of thinking to its logical conclusion, and sever the bonds they have with others as a way of avoiding potential pain.

In her final years, my sister Joyce alienated herself from almost everyone with whom she had an association. In the end, she was left with a single relationship: with herself, and that relationship was consumed by self-doubt and negativity.

Through reading the diary Joyce had left behind, I've learned that, yes, maintaining friendships is hard work, but living without close, respectful, positive, constructive relationships is way harder. How we manage these relationships, with ourselves and with others, is probably the most important factor that drives what we achieve and how we experience our lives.

Set a good example

At any point in time, you have a crazy world of different demands for your attention: the tasks you want to get done during the day, the argument you had with the kids in the morning, the notion that it always seems to be raining.

If you can easily recite a huge list of demands on yourself, it isn't a big leap to appreciate that everyone around you probably has just as complex a set of demands swirling around their heads at the moment. We all do, though we don't broadcast that fact as we are going through our lives with our masks on.

With all that baggage, it becomes difficult to be present when we are interacting with others, to be in the moment and give another person (even if it is yourself) all the attention deserved. When conversing with others, we might immediately react rather than take the time to thoughtfully respond to their needs. We might cut them off, or allow our minds to drift off to other things. Either way, that person will be less than satisfied with how they were treated. The relationship can corrode, trust may be compromised.

There is an old adage, the golden rule that says to do unto others as you would have them do unto you. For the most part, this is sage advice that works well here. Ask yourself how you would feel if you were being treated the way you treat others. Ask yourself about the outcome of those rants from your inner voice. If you don't like the potential results you see, change the behaviour accordingly.

I got into a fray recently with my son about something he did mere minutes after agreeing with me that he wouldn't do so until after he had grabbed some breakfast. The situation quickly deteriorated into a shouting match, each of us waiting only to catch our breath before unleashing the next tirade. There wasn't a great deal of listening going on, and we both thought the other person was being unreasonable.

I managed to get one thing across – that my son needed to take a break, get something to eat and cool down, then we would have a chat. That break was just as important for me as it was for him.

When we got back together, I took a different tack. Rather than barging in with continued attacks, I asked him how he felt about what was going on. I got him to tell me his story, so I could understand what was behind his actions and angry responses to what I thought were reasonable requests. There were no recriminations on my part, only requests for clarification.

The untenable argument had become a conversation. I learned critical points about why he felt the way he did, and while I could clarify his perspective in a few areas, there were others I had no idea about, and I was enlightened. I also had an opportunity to help him understand my view of the situation, and he too was able to gain some appreciative insights. We were able to resolve the issues and move on.

We all deserve a basic set of characteristics in our relationships: respect, attention, integrity, empathy. Do unto others – and yourself – as you would like others to do unto you. What you tend to get back is what you provide by example. If you think of others being caught up in a whirlwind as complex as the one you are in, it becomes easier to treat each interaction as though you are lifting and examining a piece of fine china. Relationships require patience and presence, which is best acquired through practice.

Parenting as immersive relationships

I have come to appreciate raising a family as one of the toughest projects in the world to do well. I'm amused when a well-wishing friend listens to our woes about the challenges of raising a couple of teenagers, and offers a quick sound bite of advice, like it's just that easy to fix the situation. Rarely is the advice adequate.

Families are interesting for the many dynamics that arise. For one thing, families have built into them closer connections and more stickiness than other relationships; these connections between husband and wife and parent and child are there for a long time, for better or worse. Divorce rates may be on the rise, but I still find it is a lot tougher to just write off a family relationship than it is to work our way through the challenges we face on a daily basis.

Families are also typically together more throughout the day, even if we find ourselves retreating to separate corners of the house. As parents, we have the additional responsibility of raising productive members of society. Few of us get formal training in the task, and there is no good user's manual that I have found.

As a father, I'm always trying to find the balance with my children between gentle guidance and discipline, giving them as much room to grow as I can, while making sure they don't get into trouble that is too serious – or at least not permanent, anyway.

There are times that the challenges are overwhelming, as in those early sleep-deprived days with round-the-clock feedings and diaper changes. We've learned that the tasks don't really get easier, they just get different. There are days when we want to throttle the kids – or each other, as we wrestle with our very different parenting styles.

Only after we've had a chat with friends do we see that they are going through a dance of their own, and realize that every family will have its challenges, even if what we see outside the house is that nice mask that everyone puts on. Other parents sometimes tell us we are raising the greatest two kids in the world, and my wife and I look at *their* apparently amazing kids, then ours, then each other, and give our heads a shake.

The roles in these relationships always change, depending on the current situation. There are times I need to be a provider, a protector, a guide and mentor, and a disciplinarian, all at once. Over time, I earn the opportunity to be a collaborator, a peer, sometimes even a friend. In a few years, we may experience a complete role reversal, as there is a good chance we will become dependent on our children in our later years.

For all the challenges in raising a family, we generally find that parenting is a rewarding experience, and our kids are doing fine even if they don't always meet our perfect expectations. Our relationships bring us both joy and sorrow. We couldn't truly experience that joy without the sorrow to compare it to. We can, though, continue to work our relationships so that on balance we get more of that joy part.

Nuanced roles depend on current needs

I entered the parenting game presuming that I could be a peer or friend right from the start. My kids and I would discuss or negotiate our way through every situation and life would be grand. As it turns out, with families and in life in general, one particular role, or one particular way of interacting with others, won't always be effective. In the early years, there are times when we simply have to lay down the rules, no negotiation. Dishes are to be done after meals, and they are done well or you go back and get it right. Only after the kids have mastered the basics can we start to be a little more collaborative.

How we interact with others in any relationship depends on the situation, to be sure, but it also depends on the character of the other people. On the surface, that golden rule is universal; respect and empathy should always be there. As we get to know people at a deeper level, though, we can learn more about subtle differences that lie beneath the surface.

I talked about all kinds of diversity earlier in the book. If we really understand and appreciate the differences in our fellow humans, we can take these distinctions into account as we relate with others. If they are touchy-feely people, it's worth taking the time to understand how they are feeling about a certain situation. If they are direct and to the point, they probably prefer that sort of interaction in return.

Sensitivity to the essence of people we are relating to – what makes them tick – takes serious investment in understanding them, but pays off in the depth of relationship that you can develop over time.

You reap what you sow

Whether we cultivate positive, enriching relationships or not, the results form the core of our experience in our lives. If we can appreciate that everyone has something of value to contribute to our experience, we are more apt to pay attention to each person, to take the time to understand and learn from each one.

Relationships take time to cultivate, since a major component of successful relationships is trust. Trust doesn't arrive with the flip of the switch, and each of us has our own initial trust threshold, generally a result of our past experiences. Some people may start out with a high threshold of trust, but drop it all at the first hint that they have been betrayed. Others take on more of a 'show-me' attitude. Deep trust can be decades in the making.

Solid relationships require us to overlook the perceived faults in people and focus on the strengths. We'll relate better to others if we look at the differences among us as complementary rather than a reason to avoid one another.

This investment in relationships is essential to developing resilience in our lives. Rich relationships allow us to broaden our horizons, see and experience people and events that would otherwise pass us by. Rich relationships help us grow and mature, provide objective sounding boards and different perspectives that help us see the world in a more balanced light. We gain more of those joyful moments to cherish. They form a natural safety net to help us through the challenges we will face.

If the ability to be present, to be in the moment, is a learning process, and coming up with a set of skills and practices for resilience is a gathering process, then building a solid network of relationships is a cultivating process. And the most valuable constructive relationship we can build is the relationship we have with ourselves.

Reflections

Take a quick, informal survey of the relationships in your life. Which are the ones you cherish the most, and why? Which ones are the most challenging for you to endure?

What can you do today to reinforce those great relationships and improve the challenging ones?

Consider these same questions about the relationship you have with yourself.

use your time wisely to enrich your life

Hone Your Focus

Only Then Will Your House Be Blessed – Harry Manx, 2005

In the past few chapters, we've talked about developing an ability to be present, to be in the moment, so you can thoughtfully respond to situations as they arise. We've talked about assembling a set of useful tools to help you keep fit, maintain perspective, recharge your batteries, and achieve your goals. We've talked about cultivating relationships to keep your life interesting and entertaining, and which will provide a critical safety net for times of need.

All these elements are important and valuable, but take up time in what is already a very busy day. To use strategies to build resilience, we need to make room for what's important. We need to hone our focus.

We are all familiar with the expression, "There are only twenty-four hours in a day," but in reality we've got far less time. We spend about seven hours a night sleeping. A few people can regularly make do with less sleep, and a few have the luxury of getting more, but on average that's a third of our life right there. We've all got maintenance tasks that take time in our day, from personal hygiene to keeping the house tidy. Many of us commute to work, and for most of us, a lot of what we do there wouldn't be characterized as uplifting or energizing.

If we add it up, we might have between four and ten hours a day where we can choose what we do, not the twenty-four hours we talk about. Some might call that idle time or recovery time, but I prefer to think of it as *opportunity* time.

Catching ourselves idling

As I mentioned earlier, there was a period when my wife and I found ourselves in front of the television way too much. When we describe to others how we went cold turkey to remedy our situation, some comment that they would love to have our willpower, others look at us as though we're weirdos. We've still got a television for watching movies or playing video games, but we won't let it take over our lives again.

There have been other times in my life when it wasn't clear if I was consuming alcohol, or the excessive volume was consuming me. After drinking more than my fair share and immersed in my own thoughts, the conversations with myself were rarely constructive.

Each time, I would need to break free from those downward spirals. I've learned that moderation is key.

When I was recovering from pneumonia and the death of my sister, I spent too much time brooding, sitting in front of a screen that I was barely aware of, bringing myself down. And when I did interact with others I wasn't the most pleasant person on the planet. Eventually, I hit a point where I realized this just could not go on, I had to take charge of the situation and dig myself out of that hole. For me, this took a bad experience with medications, a great deal of soul-searching, and plenty of patience and support from those around me.

We all have stories where we squander what little opportunity time we might have.

Our world promotes idling

The amount of time consumed by watching television can be frightening. Stats range from four to six hours a day per person, on average, suggesting that for everyone who spends only one hour a day watching TV, there is someone spending nine.

When we were young, we used to watch our favourite shows, but we were just as likely to head outdoors to play a game of softball or socialize. What used to be the only media escape thirty years ago has branched into many different distractions: the Internet, all the different forms of social media, and handheld devices. While we usually had to be in our living rooms to idle away the time, we can now do so in restaurants, coffee shops, bathrooms, or classrooms. The distractions are now always close at hand, and increasingly alluring.

Sure, we have access to great educational programs, and the Internet has become an indispensable resource for research and information, but the vast majority of what is consumed leans more towards entertainment than edification. All of the top-ten money-making apps at the moment on iTunes are games. Forty-four of the fifty top sellers are games, and five are social networking. The remaining one is for music sharing.

How much of our opportunity time is being consumed with this media? Do you really believe teachers have the full attention of their classes in school? We've never really had eight hours of productive time at work, and it's a safe bet we get far less today, with all these distractions. The average teenage girl will text somewhere around 3000 times a month, and I know my daughter has put that average to shame. My son consumed 100 times the data I do with his cell phone, until we sat down and clarified expectations about balance.

All these numbers are alarmingly large and end up crowding out the time we have available for doing the things that give meaning to our lives. We get a little less sleep, a little less work done, and we skip workouts because we chewed up too much time playing Angry Birds. We missed information about our math assignment in class because we were watching a viral video of someone taking a nasty spill on his bike, or looking at images of cute kittens.

Self-awareness first

Your latest phone bill may document your own time-consuming activities. If not, you can most likely identify a number of things you spend too much time doing to entertain yourself, avoid chores, or merely kill time. Some of those times you probably get upset for not accomplishing anything and scold yourself for it, grinding yourself down a notch on the self-esteem scale.

Instead, you should be happy that you noticed the problem, and consciously choose to behave differently in the future.

When most people first take stock of where their time goes, they're stunned by how much time goes down the drain. They quickly realize why their goals always seem so far out of reach. We have precious little time to do what we should be doing in life to achieve our goals. We have to take back that time from the distracters that are crowding out our opportunity time.

I used to play golf, but these days I just can't get my head around the idea of consuming four or five hours on a weekend to hit a ball around a field. Part of this is because I never got good enough to do better than losing a dozen balls and scoring well over 100. These days, though, there are too many things I find far more important and rewarding to me than golf.

Golf itself isn't all that bad. I know people who enjoy golfing regularly, who might not be as keen to be on a squash court as I am. Golf is a good way to get outdoors and cultivate relationships, and can serve the purpose of providing low-impact exercise for people. As I noted, earlier, though, tools need to resonate with you, and golf just doesn't do it for me.

If you have really clarified where you want your life to go, and have identified precisely what you want to achieve, then it is up to you to carve out the necessary time to make progress. It is up to you to exercise choice. If you want to play golf on the weekend, you will free up the time you need. So it can be for anything else you truly desire to achieve, if what you want is laid out in front of you.

Intentional use of time

We need to be conscious of where we spend our time, rather than allowing life to dictate our schedules by default. If we don't choose to do something productive, something that jazzes us, or brings us closer to the goals we want to achieve, those minutes will surely tick by. Once that minute hand swings back up to the top, that minute is behind us forever.

Choose any of the popular mantras: *seize the day, let go of the driftwood, don't sweat the small stuff*. Whatever it takes, spend a little more time intentionally working toward your desired future.

Regardless of our starting point, we all have the capacity to turn a corner and move our lives in a better direction. Once we sit down and identify what we want, what truly jazzes us, we can take steps to make that happen. We can hold onto that goal as a way of prioritizing what we do with our day. We can put aside our distractions, and really achieve great results.

Recall the last time you were headed out of town on a vacation. There is a good chance that the last two days before you left town were frenzied, as you tied up loose ends, made sure someone took care of the pets, and got that last document completed at work. When focused on a goal, especially a goal you really wanted, like a much-needed vacation, you were motivated and energized. That carrot in front of your face was what you needed to achieve your goals at a record pace.

You need a really tasty carrot dangling in front of your face to prioritize your life. You need a destination to direct your focus, whether it is a goal that helps you realize your life's ambition, or something less lofty but just as compelling, like taking a walk around the neighbourhood, starting a personal project, joining a local club. It might simply be doing anything more productive and rewarding than what is stealing away much of your time these days.

Learn to consciously choose where you spend your time. Be careful to avoid tackling too much at once, as that will lead to disappointment. Tackle these adjustments in small steps, and gradually you will see a difference; you will make a connection between exercising your choice and the new achievements you make. That new sweater will be completed, your old clothes will fit again, or you will have rekindled an old relationship.

With even such small achievements, these new activities will become habits. They will be the natural activities you reach for to fill your time, rather than those time-stealers that you leaned on in the past.

Be adaptable and balanced as you make adjustments. There will be setbacks, and there will still be occasions when you need some downtime. Sometimes you won't get done what you wanted to, and that's okay. You are heading in the right direction, and you can't always predict what will get finished in the time available. We're all optimistic about making quick headway (one of those pesky cognitive biases we have), but we can learn over time.

There's an old Polish idiom, "Nie mój cyrk, nie moje małpy". It means, "Not my circus, not my monkeys." If I don't have a role to play in its outcome, I can sit back and watch events unfold. It may not be comfortable, and I can certainly learn from it, I may even grieve about it. I will not, though, continue to be filled with remorse or regret.

Maybe a few rounds of Angry Birds will help you relax, but don't get bogged down by three hours of it. Everything in moderation, and use these distractions only as a way of recharging your batteries, rather than distracting you from your goals.

Decide on where you want to go, and head in that direction. If you make today a little bit brighter than yesterday, if you move one step closer to where you want to be, then you are doing the right things.

Choose to achieve what you want with your life, and take control of your time.

Reflections

Where did you spend your discretionary time today? What did you find yourself doing that didn't move you toward your goals or make you feel better?

Can you replace some of that time with a new hobby, energizing relationships, or activities that make you more grounded and present?

Make a few changes, and reflect on this in a week or so. Are you taking steps in the right direction?

craft the beautiful life you want

Harvest the Benefits

Here Comes The Sun – The Beatles, 1969

This book is a collection of ideas and observations that so far have served me well in my life. It is not an effortless set of steps that allows you to go on your merry way, because we live in a very complex world, and there just can't be a simple approach to navigating life, to dealing with jounce.

Just as I described four different layers of impact at the outset of this book, there are four complementary skills that, combined, form the anatomy of a life that is resilient.

This outlook, these approaches have grown and evolved organically for me over the years. Each of our lives is a work in progress, and we will continue to discover perspectives and encounter situations that challenge our current beliefs and stretch our resilience.

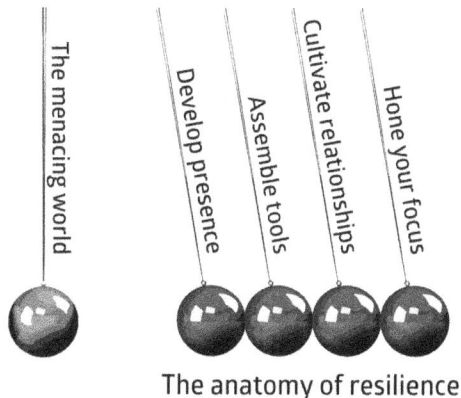

The anatomy of resilience

The menacing world · Develop presence · Assemble tools · Cultivate relationships · Hone your focus

189

This is personal

Your life is different from mine, and what works for me won't be a perfect fit for you. Take those observations, ideas, and approaches from this book that resonate for you, make them your own, and build on them. Build your own story, your own conscious path through life to deal with the difficult challenges and to experience the great experiences.

For those views that don't work for you, appreciate that I'm cool with that. I'm not asking you to mimic me; I'm suggesting we can each find our own way to deal with life through our own experiences, some introspection, and a dash of practice. Craft your own journey; the differences between your life and mine are what enrich the experience for both of us.

I believe there are some common elements between your resilient life and mine:

We can only consciously build a rich, fruitful, resilient life if we are honest with ourselves and truly understand what we believe in and stand for. We need to craft our own vision of where we want to go with our lives, be it humble or grand. We all have potential to do great things, and we need to give ourselves permission to achieve them.

We can raise our awareness and consciously choose to do more of the things that will lead us to where we want to be. We all have an opportunity to write the script for our journey and make it rich and enjoyable, knowing life will throw us roadblocks along the way. We have an opportunity to design a great life in the face of jounce. We can adjust how we observe the world, how we use our precious time, and how we interact with others. These are our raw materials, we need to use them responsibly and with purpose.

When we adjust our outlook on the world, the world will indeed change how it interacts with us. Certainly, as we interact with others in an appreciative, respectful way, we will get more of the same in return. I believe, from experience, this extends out to the rest of the universe as well. If I can appreciate the beauty and wonder of the universe for what it is, rather than trying to bend it to my selfish wishes, my experience with the universe improves, and this informs and reinforces my fundamental beliefs that guide my life.

This journey starts within you. There is plenty within each of us that can be adjusted, managed, or consciously tweaked to provide a better perspective and outlook. With that approach, we don't need anyone's cooperation to make great strides. Until we have made these internal adjustments, it is fruitless to try to push others to adapt to us.

This journey never ends

All this effort, this lifetime of managing our perspective and adjusting our goals and behaviours, is still not a guarantee of a great, wonderful, perfect life. Indeed, we should all expect that we will continue to face challenges. For all of us, there will be times when we struggle, stumble, and fall. There will be times that we weep, that we suffer losses.

When I was a child I lost my best buddy, Billy Walker. I was fortunate to rebound from that loss fairly quickly. Later, when my sister Joyce passed away, the recovery felt much more difficult. Over time, I've come to appreciate that we can consciously develop skills and attitudes that make us more resilient.

Taking this conscious approach will help us manage what life throws at us more effectively. With a clear outlook and wider range of tools to work through life, we will get past the little speed bumps faster. We will be better equipped to climb out of the depths of despair with a richer set of resources and a stronger, appreciative network of friends to lean on.

We will create more of the good times in our lives, too. We will achieve more of our life-long goals, and our daily existence will be enriched with closer friends, a more positive outlook, and rewarding experiences.

Our lives are very complex, and always changing. We could easily be overwhelmed by the magnitude of this task, but don't despair. Think of this book as a rough map scrawled on the back of a napkin, revealing to you that there might be something worth looking for – a treasure map of sorts. Build clarity around what your treasure looks like, learn the skills to map out how to find that treasure.

Live your life to the fullest. Take small steps in the right direction, harvest those benefits, take the next steps. Always learn, grow, and adjust. Gradually become more aware, more intentional, more resilient.

This is about all of us

All this may appear to be my way of dealing with the crap that life throws at me, my way of surviving against being jounced around. It is this, and more.

For all of the issues I described in the first section of this book that are harbingers of despair, there are just as many bright lights in this world: an expanding awareness of the frailty of the planet, and the challenges we face in sustaining our world, even as severe climate events escalate; a deeper understanding of the relationships between corporations and governments and the distribution of power and wealth, even if the balance continues to tip in the wrong direction; a stronger appreciation of the need for all of us to find a way to live together in peace on this increasingly overcrowded planet, even as conflict remains a concern in many areas; a growing body of knowledge and invention to address the challenges we face; a growing movement toward awareness and action to allow us to sustain and grow our ability to thrive as a species.

We are at a crossroads on this planet; some might call it a struggle between good and evil. We may see significant change in the very near future, or the world may slowly, gradually lean a bit more in one direction or another over time. In either case, there are more factors than ever that could cause the balance to tip one way or the other.

When we talk about resilience, about dealing with jounce, we are more than merely talking about getting through life in one piece.

If we are concerned about greater issues than getting through the day, if we want to make a difference and do what we can to tip the balance in the right direction, I believe that building personal resilience is a critical first step in that direction.

If we have a well-grounded outlook and an effectively considered approach to life, we have the ability to make a difference in a broader sense. We are better equipped to be one of those bright lights that takes action to change the world.

I've learned I can be a brighter light as a husband, as a father, as a family member, even as a coach and facilitator with clients. Being in better control of my life allows me the space to be able to support others. Over time, the circle of influence can continue to grow. We aren't all destined to be a Nelson Mandela or a Richard Branson, or whoever you look up to as a heroic figure, but we can develop the capacity to consciously move in that direction. We can all be a positive force in our own lives, the lives of the people around us, and the world.

I urge you to make a choice today, craft the future you want and build the capability to get there. Start by making a difference to that one floundering starfish you can save: yourself.

A fulfilled and resilient life grows from this.

Chapter Notes

Here, after the fact, are some models I have used to help me understand what I experience, along with some other pointers and perspectives for additional reading.

I've provided general search topics instead of specific links to articles. This eliminates the concern that a link may no longer be valid when you follow it, and gives you access to more up-to-date information as it becomes available. On the downside, though, this information hasn't been vetted and may be misleading, or in the fullness of time, may be found to be incorrect. Exercise caution and judgment; cross-reference and compare different sources; and form your own balanced opinion on each of these topics. Explore uncharted territory; you will find nuggets of information I'm not aware of.

Billy Walker

Over dinner with a friend recently, I mentioned that I was writing this book, and that ideally it might lead to an opportunity to speak to others about what's in these pages. He said, "Wait a minute…I know the arc of this story!" and he went on to describe how most 'inspirational' speakers talk about personal tragedies and *their* journey to overcome these tragedies. Certainly, I lead with a story about personal tragedy here, even if I wasn't the one who suffered the most in that case.

What's important, though, is that everyone has a story, and most of us can relate to these stories with one of our own. The goal in this book is to get you to think about *your* story, *your* life. The anecdotes I provide here are merely examples to illustrate the points. Don't worry about me or applaud how I make my way through my life; work on building your own rich journey.

In the midst of writing this book, I came across psychiatrist Viktor E. Frankl's book, *Man's Search for Meaning*. There aren't too many stories more harrowing than Frankl's description of his experience in Nazi death camps. His story informs his own world view, which he describes in the second half of his book as the theory of *logotherapy*. There are many ideas that parallel his thoughts in this book, though this hasn't been codified into a formal theory.

Search terms, further reading: Viktor Frankl, Man's Search for Meaning, logotherapy

The World Is Changing

There are many potential sources of challenges we face that I haven't even touched on in the chapter.

We see global struggles based on opposing political structures or religious beliefs, and local protests such as the Arab Spring and the Occupy Movement, that reflect the difficulties of governing a diverse set of needs.

We are learning the extent to which governments are spying on each other and on their citizens, as the people who attempt to raise awareness of these issues are ignored or held up as traitors.

Many people are seeing reason for concern, even reason for panic. For those you might deem as Chicken Littles for their sense of urgency, there are others who refuse to accept the evidence given and see a great future ahead. I believe the truth about which challenges will become critical and when lies somewhere in the middle of those extremes, but there is enough evidence for me to fear for my children's future. What actually happens will only be clear in the rear-view mirror of our lives.

For a frightening look at how we are currently contributing to what could potentially be the largest die-off of species ever, read *The Sixth Extinction* by Elizabeth Kolbert. This book provides a stark context for what is primarily a human-centric narrative in this book.

Search terms, further reading: Edward Snowden, Occupy Movement, ogallala aquifer depletion, Energy Skeptic, James Kunstler, Michael Ruppert, Ray Kurzweil, The Sixth Extinction

Our Failing Institutions

There is plenty of information online about the immense growth of the drug industry and the questionable practices of many of the major manufacturers. This is primarily driven by the corporate bias toward stakeholder value and the massive costs of bringing a new drug to market, rather than the benefit to the consumer of these medications. Stakeholder value and customer benefit shouldn't be at odds, but when they are, the choice rarely benefits the customer.

The concerns I raise about the limits of modern medicine come from my scientific background and recognition that, historically, we have always been arrogant about our current knowledge being definitive. We have our current set of 'the world is flat' presumptions that will seem ridiculous in the future. Lewis Thomas has written a number of engaging books about medical progress, generally from the glowing perspective of a proud parent. As a parent myself, I'm aware of my bias to downplay the flaws in my children.

I don't believe we understand well enough how the brain works to be messing with it as we do; the stakes are too high. Yes, there are some people who benefit from appropriate use of medication, but there are many others who are not adequately managed within the complex system. Again, the primary motivators are misdirected: dealing with an apparently overwhelming burden with insufficient resources, the human tendency is to choose an expedient solution.

We know about banks deemed too big to fail that have been exposed for fraudulent schemes of manipulating value for their benefit and increasing the size and frequency of bubbles in the stock markets, eroding our confidence in these systems. Despite the evidence of the intentional approach for these schemes, few perpetrators have been chastised for their actions, and little changes.

Search terms, further reading: Medication Madness, Pfizer fines, The Truth About Drug Companies, The Youngest Science, Antidepressant Use, too big to fail, The Corporation

Dealing with Others

Albert Mehrabian published his study about communication and the importance of words, tone, and body language when speaking. There have been disputes about the methodology of his work and the limitations of his findings, but I doubt that any of us would disagree with the general notion of how we lose nuance as we constrain the approach to communicating information.

With today's tendency to lean on constrained forms of communication, more people are uncomfortable with extended face-to-face communication or even phone calls. As society moves in this general direction, we are preventing ourselves from enjoying full, empathic dialogue. We may be conversing more, but we are communicating less.

An interesting perspective on how we interact with one another comes from religious scholar James P. Carse's book, *Finite and Infinite Games*. He describes two approaches people take: some people interact in a finite game, where they are trying to win, others interact in a game where they are trying to maintain a sustained interaction. Finite games are sometimes appropriate, but not always necessary.

Search terms, further reading: Albert Mehrabian, forms of communication, empathy vs. sympathy, James P. Carse, Finite and Infinite Games

Anywhere, Anytime, Anyhow

Gone are the days when we can simply drill a quick well and have oil push its own way out of the ground for us to exploit. The term *peak oil* is used to describe the point where any new energy we get out of the ground will be increasingly difficult and expensive to obtain. Before today, there was no economic or environmental sense to access the bitumen in the tar sands of Northern Alberta or to frack for natural gas. From now on, satisfying our thirst for petroleum-based energy will continue to be more difficult, expensive, and environmentally damaging.

People have always looked for novel ways of exploiting existing infrastructures for their own profit. By accessing paths that provide information mere nanoseconds faster than other people would get that information, flash trading is giving some an unfair advantage in the stock market. *Flash Boys* exposes how technology can be used, and how difficult it can be to maintain a level playing field.

That building in Vancouver constructed to withstand earthquakes is called the Qube, and was built in 1969. It was originally an office tower, and has been recently converted to luxury condominiums to feed the burgeoning residential real-estate market.

Search terms, further reading: peak oil, Flash Boys, the Qube Vancouver

Evolution

I first learned about psychotherapist Virginia Satir's work through an adaptation of her Change Process Model in a business context. A few years later I participated in a guided meditation, facilitated by one of her colleagues, and it was one of the most spiritually fulfilling experiences in my life. The foundation of her work centres around human validation and acceptance, two powerful concepts that can serve as guideposts in almost any situation.

The body of work in the area of cognitive biases is both deep and wide, and it all boils down to the fact that we tend to oversimplify what we see in a huge variety of ways, and this gets us into trouble. What once served us well is becoming dodgy. I fear that I am guilty of applying the 'IKEA effect' to the context of the musical instruments I build. The bottom line here is that if we are conscious that these biases exist, and learn to observe them in action (as in that marshmallow experiment), we can lean more on our pre-frontal cortex to make better decisions.

Search terms, further reading: Virginia Satir, Satir change process model, cognitive bias mitigation, Walter Mischel, marshmallow experiment

Diversity

While we lived in Southern Ontario, my father commuted to Michigan for work, and during the 1967 race riots in Detroit (one of many examples of such tension), he drove right through the riot zone every day – with his doors locked, and not really stopping at intersections. I was really too young at the time to truly understand what was going on. There remain far too many examples of racial tension in the world, the underpinnings of anything from war and genocide to more benign forms of prejudice that lead us to simply avoid others because they are *different*.

In my experience working and travelling in many parts of the world and interacting with many people who are different from me, I have found that even if there are overall perceptions that bias my thinking in the wrong direction, everyone I have met and interacted with has been wonderful.

There is a wide range of personality tests (though often called 'tests', they are better described as inventories, to avoid the notion there is a 'right answer') that allow us to explore diversity in how we interpret the world and interact with others. I'm most familiar with the Strength Deployment Inventory (or SDI), but most people recognize the Myers-Briggs Type Inventory as one they have been exposed to. As with any tool, these can be used inappropriately, and my experience with Myers-Briggs is that people tend to take the superficial results to put others in boxes; I'm an *INTJ* in that model, and for some people that's all they want to know. There's great value in guidance from someone who's well versed in the underlying models.

Rather than simply categorizing others, these instruments should be used to start conversations to better understand one another, to appreciate our differences as strengths, and as in Virginia Satir's work, focus on validation and acceptance of who we are. The magic in these instruments is that they expose a form of diversity that is generally not observed or consciously considered, and there is as much self-discovery as there is a deeper understanding of others.

Search terms, further reading: race riots, Myers-Briggs, Strength Deployment Inventory, personality tests

Complexity

The butterfly effect comes from an area of science called *chaos theory*, which looks at the detailed interactions of the world at a very small scale to see how they impact the results that we can all see and feel. It's an interesting example of how we can push the limits of science to better understand the world around us, even if the term actually comes from a computational error in the model.

That starfish story has been used in many contexts over the years, and is one of the more heavily relied on stories for inspirational quotes on the Web. You've probably seen it before; it is most commonly attributed to anthropologist and natural science writer Loren Eiseley, and adapted from his book, *The Star Thrower*. I think the idea of becoming a star thrower is a nice metaphor to guide our lives.

My first foray into post-secondary education was systems engineering at the University of Waterloo, and even though I didn't make it past second year, the overall concept of systems left its mark on my way of looking at the world. I see many examples that reinforce the idea that simple models cannot possibly explain much of what happens around us; life is far too complex. With all that, though, we can look at this bigger picture to understand feedback loops and proximity to choose how to act to make a difference.

Consultant Gerald M. Weinberg's book, *An Introduction to General Systems Thinking*, originally came out in 1975 and remains popular today. It's a digestible view of how we can take some of the principles of systems to become more effective thinkers. It was at his "Amplifying Your Effectiveness" conference that I participated in that guided meditation by one of Virginia Satir's colleagues. While it doesn't appear that the conference has been run for the past several years, there remains a wealth of articles online. This was the least technical conference attended by techies that I've ever been to, and was by far the most rewarding.

Search terms, further reading: chaos theory, butterfly effect, Loren Eiseley, Amplify Your Effectiveness, Gerald M. Weinberg, systems thinking

Addictions

There are plenty of articles today that focus on childhood obesity and mortality and food addiction, with groups such as the CDC and the Public Health Agency of Canada weighing in on the matter. There are many examples of how we can become addicted to things other than drugs, alcohol, and gambling and how grave the impact can be. Those big three remain huge concerns, but we need to dramatically widen the scope of our thinking.

The prescribing of off-label medications is generally legal and is a far more common practice than most of us realize. When the medical community chooses to do this, it is called off-label medication; if the consumer chooses to do this, it is labelled as prescription drug abuse. Risk rises if medications are used in ways that haven't been carefully vetted by rigorous trials, which are notoriously expensive and time consuming for the drug companies. If there are tradeoffs between profit and safety, where is the balancing point?

Even worse are companies that understand the mechanisms of addiction and exploit them explicitly to their advantage. There are many cases where advances in science are definitely not being used for the greater good.

Search terms, further reading: childhood obesity addiction, off-label medication, prescription drug abuse, video game addiction

Stress

There are many resources on the Web for dealing with stress. A common theme for many of these resources is to lean on a number of different techniques as a comprehensive strategy for living a stress-free life.

The first step for dealing with stress, though, is to see the signs. We used those biodots in the workshops at the Crisis Centre, and they are available for purchase over the Web, but there are other signs to be aware of that don't need external tools.

Here's as good a place as any for a blatant plug for organizations like the Crisis Centre. Most urban areas have some form of crisis centre. They provide information through public outreach, participate in valuable studies, and often run a phone or Web-based help line to support those who need immediate help to get through what they are facing. The Crisis Centre I was involved with (formally known as the Crisis Intervention and Suicide Prevention Centre of BC) is primarily volunteer run, and provides a huge service to the community. These volunteers are rigorously trained before working with the public, and bring along a whole lot of empathy for their role. Get to know the resources you have available locally, spend some time volunteering if you have a chance, and don't be afraid to reach out to them if you need to.

Search terms, further reading: stress management, stress signs, biodots, crisis centre

Despair

I carefully skirted around naming this chapter "Suicide". While that was one of the main precursors to my writing this book, I have come to the opinion that the emphasis needs to be broader and more positive than this worst-case ending. The term *suicide* immediately sets a particular scene for most people, and to even have that word in the table of contents would make this a 'suicide book' in the minds of some.

That stated, suicide is a significant issue that we can't ignore. Causes are multiplying, the rates are increasing in many areas, and we cannot treat this as that-which-shall-not-be-named. It needs to be faced head-on, and I have found that talking about it, just as Harry Potter was not afraid to discuss Voldemort, has been the most therapeutic activity for me to better deal with the issue.

I'm pretty sure that I encountered Elizabeth Kübler-Ross and her book, *On Death and Dying*, after Billy Walker passed away, and I learned about those five stages of grief in her model: denial, anger, bargaining, depression and acceptance. Over the years, as I started to deploy different models to describe situations, I have learned that the real world is far more nuanced than most models might imply. We may be able to see these stages of grief, but likely some more strongly than others, some without any clear, overt signals at all. I believe the model holds for a variety of situations around loss and grief, and the best way to address these situations based on this model is to be consciously proactive at working through the stages. We want to get to the point of acceptance as aggressively as possible, and it is dangerous to simply wait for the stages to progress on their own. Sometimes they just don't.

Search terms, further reading: suicide stats, Elizabeth Kübler-Ross, On Death and Dying, five stages of grief

Embrace the Journey

There are a few different approaches you can take to producing a timeline of your life: the simple meandering line I talk about in the book; cataloguing and plotting significant events on a timeline; purchasing and maintaining a specially designed poster that lays out your life week by week over ninety years so you can see your whole history in great detail. Any of these is reasonable if it drives you to reflect on where you have been.

That Edison story comes from a book called *Virtuoso Teams*, by Andy Boynton and Bill Fischer. The book provides a wide variety of anecdotes about great teams in a wide range of domains, and reinforces the point that if we collaborate well together, the whole is definitely greater than the sum of the parts.

William Ford Gibson's quote about the future rings true every day in the news. Today the people in Toledo, Ohio, can't drink their tap water, Nigerian armies are being accused of atrocities just as horrible as those being committed by their enemies, the Ebola virus is running out of control in West Africa, California is quickly running out of water, war is escalating in the Middle East and in Ukraine. Dozens of similar stories have been pushed off the front pages. People around the world right now are dealing with situations that could impact each of us some time in the future. It can be useful to watch and learn, as events unfold around us.

Search terms, further reading: life timeline, life calendar, Virtuoso Teams, William Ford Gibson

Commit to the Effort

The Satir change model comes into play again here. The turning point in the model, where change really starts to occur and becomes different from all the false starts we are familiar with when we try to lose some weight or quit smoking, is where we connect the change in behaviour with that better future that we see. When we can appreciate that it's easier to climb that flight of steps when we've smoked less, or when we've snacked on fruit rather than doughnuts, that connection reinforces the behaviour and we're on the way to true change.

That connection needs to be conscious, and this brings us back to how we have evolved and the notion that our conscious brain is generally lazy. Without the effort to make connections like this, we won't be training ourselves to behave differently. With that effort, over time, these behaviours become the new normal, and become our unconscious choice.

Much of the literature around making choices and changing behaviours touches on these ideas. There are many decision-making approaches that are used in the business context, and a central theme behind them is to make the decision a rational one. Despite what we might like to believe, we are generally not rational decision makers.

Search terms, further reading: decision making, making a choice, rational thought

Foster Your Convictions

A number of different theories are being used to describe the distance and size of quasars, but the one I described in this chapter seems to be the most prominent theory in use today. I don't know if the approach has become more rigorous over the years since I was exposed to it in university; at the time there was certainly sufficient reason to be skeptical. I think there is great value in being skeptical about many things we are being told these days.

The book that easily had the strongest influence on me in the 80s was *Gödel, Escher, Bach*, written by cognitive science professor Douglas Hofstadter. It was an extremely challenging read, with interconnections at so many levels that there remain new nuggets of insight that I can still derive from it today. One of the themes in the book was the exploration of Gödel's *incompleteness* theorem. While deeply mathematical in nature, what it drove home for me was the conclusion that we can't possibly completely understand ourselves – nor, by extension, our convictions – because we are inside that system. I'm pretty sure I've made as many leaps of faith in this conclusion as they have about the distance of quasars.

Search terms, further reading: distance of quasars, Douglas Hofstadter, Gödel Escher Bach

Craft a Destination

Jim Collins and Jerry I. Porras' book, *Built to Last*, describes that Big Hairy Audacious Goal that is a key distinction of those corporations that have shown sustained results better than the average. Jim Collins followed up with another book, *Good to Great*, that described how companies can make the transition to greatness.

I'm not keen on the meticulous application of business models to the personal world, but there are certainly some ideas that have merit to reflect on. Corporations, by their very nature, are strongly biased toward success in terms of things like shareholder value and profits, where I believe we need to be thinking personally about a broader definition of what success means for each of us. The common kernel that we can glean from these books is to have that clear vision of the future, that BHAG, though framing it in terms of monetary success is not the most important dimension to consider.

In Chris Hadfield's book, which came out after he completed his round as the commander of the International Space Station, he provides a lucid example of a BHAG that he formulated as a young child. It's an engaging book with an engrossing story, the key point being that Chris' vision of what's important isn't a self-serving corporate-like vision, but one for humanity in general. I guess you would get that perspective after seeing from way out in space that the earth looks like such a fragile ball. In James P. Carse's terminology, Chris Hadfield is playing an infinite game.

After reading Chris' book, it's pretty clear I didn't have the right stuff to be an astronaut back when I applied for the job.

Search terms, further reading: Jim Collins, Jerry I. Porras, Built to Last, Good to Great, Chris Hadfield, An Astronaut's Guide to Life on Earth

Know Your Starting Point

Robert Fritz developed the model for Structural Tension Charting, where we develop a rich view of our preferred future, capture where we are now, and use the gap between them as a way of creating a tension that we release by doing what is required to narrow that gap. Again, if I were to lead with that model, I expect many readers would roll their eyes. Instead, we merely have to see that having a vision isn't enough if we don't have a starting point to work from. It makes sense to be honest with ourselves about where we are now.

I'm an analytical person, so I actually sit down and follow a written process to take these steps – preferred future, current point, steps to narrow the gap – but that is definitely not everyone's cup of tea. What's important is to simply make sure you don't ignore any of these areas, and it helps to think about these things in this order, as one leads logically to the next. Reflect on this process periodically; that's why writing it down is important to me, at my age.

Search terms, further reading: Robert Fritz, The Path of Least Resistance for Managers

Develop an Ability To Be Present

Mihaly Csikszentmihalyi's book, *Finding Flow*, is a quick read and a great introduction to the concept of flow. There are other resources that talk specifically about flow in particular domains, such as professional sports, that you might find useful.

Mindfulness was the centerpiece of the workshops we ran at the Crisis Centre, based on the work of professor John Kabat-Zinn. Our approach in gaining mindfulness was based on guided meditations, all geared toward calming oneself and learning to be in the present. There are many variations on meditations that can work in this way, such as Zen-based meditation, and that Satir-based meditation I was involved in a few years back did the same thing. Meditation brings calmness, calm brings focus, focus allows us to find flow. I've experienced a few magical flow moments in my life, and continue to strive for more.

Multitasking seems to be the opposite end of the spectrum from finding flow, and I'm not aware of any study that suggests you can do several things simultaneously without sacrificing quality or actually taking more time. If you have a number of things you want to achieve, decide on the order you want to do them in, and focus on one at a time.

Search terms, further reading: Mihaly Csikszentmihalyi, Finding Flow, mindfulness, John Kabat-Zinn, Zen, multitasking cognition

Assemble a Set of Tools

There is no limit to the tools you can add to your toolkit. I'm sure you already have a few you lean on. Look at what others do around you, look at your goals in life, and ask yourself what skills you might need to acquire to achieve these goals, or search any of the criteria I identified in this chapter to come up with new ideas.

Watch for what is happening in your neighbourhood and at community centres, find places to volunteer your time, look for Meetup Groups in your area that you think might be fun. Take courses in areas that interest you.

Keep searching, keep adding tools to your repertoire, and have fun doing it.

Search terms, further reading: relaxing activities, Meetup, community centre programs, (your city) volunteering

Cultivate Relationships

Very often, leadership is a term used for relationships where there is some form of hierarchy, such as a parent-child or boss-employee relationship. Thought of that way, leadership is often interpreted as getting people to do your bidding.

I prefer to use the term *influence* rather than *leadership*, as it takes away that bias towards being in charge. Anyone can influence anyone else in a relationship, by using many of the skills that are often attributed to leadership. If one of my children wants me to buy into something they want to do, they can influence me to do so, even against the grain of that hierarchy that exists. We can all lead at times.

When we do lead, we all tend to have our preferred approach. Your preferred style may be to simply tell others what they need to do; or you might try to negotiate cooperation; or you may simply delegate responsibility to others. Ken Blanchard and Paul Hersey describe a Situational Leadership Theory, a model that says it is best to use a leadership style based on the readiness of the followers – are they able, willing, and secure in their ability to do what they are being asked to do? I've found that model useful to reflect on as a parent, allowing me to choose when it makes sense to simply explain what I want done, or when it is safe to delegate responsibilities for activities. It extends nicely to all relationships, particularly if we think *influencing* rather than *leading*.

Search terms, further reading: Kenneth Blanchard, Paul Hersey, situational leadership

Hone Your Focus

There are a number of resources that describe the time we spend in idle activities. While any statistics – particularly on the Internet from an unvetted source – should be taken with a grain of salt, the general trend is that many of us are spending more time overall in these activities, and we need to consciously claw back our time. In the workplace, email is both an essential tool and a consumer of time. The number of ways our time can be stolen from us will only be increasing.

There are a number of systems that people use to gain control over how their time is spent. I've been very happy with the approach suggested by David Allen in his book, *Getting Things Done*, and there is a huge cult of GTD practitioners and tools you can use to implement these strategies.

I've also learned from Steve Prentice's book, *Cool Time*, that there is great value in carving out some blocks of time for yourself, to do some strategic thinking or make progress on things you want to get done. He calls these blocks *keystone time*, like that block at the top of those ancient arches that holds the whole thing together.

Search terms, further reading: time watching TV, video game usage, alcohol consumption, Internet usage, David Allen, Getting Things Done, GTD, Steve Prentice, Cool Time

Acknowledgements

My name is on the cover of this book, but a book rarely comes to fruition without significant help from others along the way.

Gary Robinson introduced many of these ideas to me in the context of teams and projects, knowing darned well these ideas work because they resonate at a personal level first.

Marina Ma helped me realize this really isn't my book after all, giving me the permission I needed to let it go. All I'm really doing here is playing my notes, with hope that these notes resonate in some parts of the universe.

Patrick Conroy explored cognitive biases as part of his research, and this topic generated many lively discussions over coffee.

Les Kletke showed me that his system for writing a book actually does ease the pain of getting the story out on the table, and he let me know that the story has already made a difference in one starfish's life.

Lois Braun provided the objective feedback that helped me convert my rough story into a structured, presentable form. She did this in a way that didn't make me feel like my baby was ugly, which is an art form of its own.

Along with Les and Lois, Paul Krahn and Elizabeth Falk round out the publishing team from Manitoba, helping develop a visually clean and tidy book.

As always, my wife Winney has been here to support me through projects like this, long before they look like a project, even when they conflict with the home renovation constantly on the go.

There are many others who have contributed in some way for this book, far too numerous to mention. They have all, through their interaction with me, shaped me in some way to be who I am, and hence shaped this book to be what it is. To everyone along the way, thank you.

About the Author

Jim Brosseau's career and life have meandered in many interesting ways. He grew up wanting to be a surgeon, but changed his mind just before entering university. He ended up with a degree in physics, but never used that knowledge in the real world.

His work has varied from involvement in a monumental air traffic control system to many simpler projects with small teams. He has worked with and taught topics from high technology to personal relationships, engaging with high school students and CEOs alike, and has learned from everyone he's come in contact with along the way. For the most part, he's never stayed with any one organization for more than a few years; the call to do something different has always been strong for Jim.

He is now acting on one of the most important changes in his personal life: answering the call to raise awareness about resilience, turning up the volume on the discussion about how we can consciously build our resilience, at a time when the need is more acute than ever.

Jim lives with his wife and two children in Vancouver, coaches and trains teams to become more effective at working together, and hopes to be competent in both building and playing stringed instruments some day. It's all part of his journey.

www.ingramcontent.com/pod-product-compliance
Lightning Source LLC
Chambersburg PA
CBHW021140090426
42740CB00008B/866

9 780099 390 3106